BEYOND BORDERS

PROFILES IN INTERNATIONAL EDUCATION

JOSEPH S. JOHNSTON, JR.
Vice President for Programs
Association of American Colleges

RICHARD J. EDELSTEIN
Director of Professional Development
and International Affairs
American Assembly of Collegiate Schools of Business

D0681321

ASSOCIATION OF AMERICAN COLLEGES AND
AMERICAN ASSEMBLY OF COLLEGIATE SCHOOLS
OF BUSINESS, 1993

THIS WORK WAS SUPPORTED BY
THE KPMG PEAT MARWICK FOUNDATION

Published by
Association of American Colleges
1818 R Street, N.W.
Washington, D.C. 20009

ISBN 0-911696-60-1
Library of Congress Catalog No. 93-71472

CONTENTS

ACKNOWLEDGMENTS

The authors wish to express their special gratitude to:

The KPMG Peat Marwick Foundation
William K. Laidlaw, Jr.
and Jane Spalding

They also acknowledge with thanks the contributions of:
Charles Hickman
Andrew Seely
Sharon Barber
Paula Brownlee
Nancy Albert
Nora Topalian
Joann Stevens
David Stearman
Cynthia Olson
Stephen Taylor

and all those involved with the AAC/AACSB projects on internationalizing the curriculum through business-liberal arts cooperation.

BEYOND BORDERS

BY JOSEPH S. JOHNSTON, JR.

Borders are useful—even necessary. They tell us where one thing ends and another begins. They tell us who claims what and how far those claims extend. In a sense, they tell us what is our business and what is the business of others. They help us organize our world, which without them would be a muddle.

We can respect borders too much, however. After all, many are essentially arbitrary, imposed by force, historical accident, or unhappy compromise. Many exist despite—indeed, often in defiance of—commonalities between and among the realms they separate. They divide common ground. They discourage travel, frustrate discourse, and impede understanding. Borders can be geographical or disciplinary; in either case, when there is work to be accomplished, it is important to keep them from getting in the way.

A massive challenge now confronts American higher education: the challenge of internationalization. Our colleges and universities must become environments of teaching and learning—as well as research and service—that reflect and address the increasingly interdependent nature of our world. Their success with internationalization—"arguably the most powerful substantive redirection in the history of American higher education"[1]—will depend on their ability to get beyond borders—both the literal, geopolitical ones that demarcate nation-states and the figurative (and often less permeable) ones that define the academic disciplines. Hence the title of this publication.

The particular initiatives profiled within these pages exemplify interdisciplinary collaboration in the service of international education. In 1987, two national associations, rooted in the worlds of arts and sciences and business education, respectively, began a joint examination of the opportunities for collaboratively internationalizing these two areas—and higher education as a whole. Beginning in 1988, the Association of American Colleges (AAC) and the American Assembly of Collegiate Schools of Business (AACSB) received a series of grants from the KPMG Peat Marwick Foundation. The first grant supported an invitational conference in June 1988 in Montvale, New Jersey, which brought together business and liber-

Globalization is here to stay, and its pace in
the foreseeable future will only accelerate.
Increasingly, the expansion of the international
dimension of higher education is not so much
an option as a responsibility

---

al arts faculty members and administrators from twenty colleges and universities. The second and third grants made possible three similarly designed regional conferences in 1990 in Montvale; Chicago; and Scottsdale, Arizona, and a concluding national conference in Lincolnshire, Illinois. Most recently, a fourth KPMG Peat Marwick Foundation grant funded a small competition through which eighteen institutions have been awarded seed money for collaborative initiatives in the international arena.

This same grant supports this publication. Primarily a set of program descriptions, it is intended to suggest the many different ways in which internationally minded faculty members and administrators can—and have begun to—get beyond borders. It summarizes experience and insight that might be helpful to others, whatever their disciplinary homes.

Programs of many types are featured here, but initiatives resulting from the cooperation of arts and sciences and business programs are particularly well represented. In part, this reflects this publication's auspices. It also reflects our belief that programs in these two well-enrolled domains can and must help one another in their respective efforts to internationalize. Entire institutions benefit when business and liberal arts programs find common cause in developing global dimensions. Presidents, deans, and other academic leaders can find in these alliances some of their most powerful and effective agents of institution-wide, globally oriented change.

BACKGROUND

Few people need to be persuaded that it is important to make our colleges and universities more international. In so many realms, the very distinction between the domestic and the international seems to be disappearing. The United States, Richard Lambert points out, is becoming "a permanent multicultural society in which the world is us, not some distant backdrop."[2] We are connected with distant peoples as never before by economics, politics, transportation, and telecommunication, and we face with them a host of issues and problems—disease, hunger, military conflict, environmental degradation—that transcend national and regional borders. Globalization is here to stay, and its pace in the foreseeable future will only accelerate. Increasingly, the expansion of the international dimension of higher education is not so much an option as a responsibility—for all institutions and for all programs within them.

◆

Of course, calls for internationalization are not new. The rationales put forward, however, have changed significantly over the years—as have their impact on higher education. The first substantive pressures for U.S. colleges and universities to develop more international expertise emerged after World War II in response to arguments of national security and international political advantage arising from this country's new-found role as "leader of the free world." With major funding from sources such as the U.S. Agency for International Development (AID), the National Defense Education Act (NDEA), the Fulbright Scholar Program, and private foundations, universities were especially successful in developing centers of international expertise—particularly area studies and language programs— and involving faculty members in technical and developmental assistance programs overseas. Although impressive, this activity was oriented largely to the graduate-level production of specialists and did little to make entire institutions more international in character or outlook.[3]

The 1970s and 1980s witnessed a stepping back from international concerns. The country became leery of foreign entanglements after the Vietnam War, and federal and private support for international education declined. Symptomatically, between 1967 and 1987, the number of undergraduates majoring in a foreign language shrank by one-half.[4] Starting from what had been exceedingly low levels, study abroad did make gains during the late 1980s, and foreign student enrollments burgeoned—but again without occasioning any fundamental change in the institutions that received them.[5]

The economic competitiveness concerns that colleges and universities recognize as their primary mandate for change in the 1990s began to take shape a decade earlier. In 1979, the federal Commission on Foreign Language and International Study issued an influential report documenting the low level of American students' competency in foreign languages and their weak grasp of world affairs.[6] By the mid-1980s, the worsening balance-of-trade crisis had brought the issue of U.S. competitiveness to the fore; business and political leaders began focusing on improving the educational system as a necessary part of the solution.

Stunned by the dismal performance of U.S. elementary and secondary students on comparative tests of academic proficiency, policy makers at every level called for dramatic improvements in science and math, particularly. To many, however, the link was becoming clear as well between America's economic woes and its failure to teach its citizens foreign lan-

We have been slow to recognize and respond to
the increasing interconnectedness of the world
we find ourselves facing

---

guages and educate them about geography, world history, other cultures,
the workings of the international economy, and global politics.[7] Congress
provided new support in the 1980s for as many as one hundred university-
based area studies centers; in addition, through Title VIB of the Higher Education Act, Centers for International Business Education and Research began working in close association with them. At the state level, too, there
was a new recognition of the economic benefit of international education,
which governors strongly endorsed "as a way to bring more jobs and income, by enabling workers to produce goods that are salable on the world
market."[8]

Perhaps in part because students began to see their own economic
self-interest in international education, the late 1980s and early 1990s
have brought higher enrollments in language programs and other internationally oriented courses and a continued steady increase in undergraduate
study abroad. These and other "demand side" trends, including the growth
in the number of students from other countries attending U.S. institutions, have by themselves given many American campuses a more international character.

On the "supply side," however, relatively few institutions have
changed policies and programs in coherent or effective ways. Internationalization has been likened to that earlier reinvention of the intellectual
framework, the scientific revolution; it is "a disorderly development, lacking clear definition, boundaries and agreement."[9] As institutions attempt
to incorporate global perspectives into their programs, their efforts tend
naturally to be scattered and tentative. Yet as Crauford Goodwin and
Michael Nacht point out, the internationalization required at this time is
"far more profound than that accomplished in earlier decades."[10] It will
not be the kind of change that can be left to a slow and natural process
of evolution. It will require, on campus after campus, commitment to an
institution-wide policy and sustained execution of a well-conceived plan.
We turn, then, to two large questions: What kind of rationale can and
should secure such a commitment? What are the elements that might
constitute such a plan?

RATIONALES FOR INTERNATIONALIZATION

Today, the dominant argument for internationalizing higher education is
that it will ensure the nation's economic competitiveness. This argument
has considerable force. It touches all Americans and evokes a certain ur-

gency. Our geographical isolation, self-sufficiency in natural resources, and abundant internal markets have made us, as a nation, uncommonly independent.[11] We have been slow to recognize and respond to the increasing interconnectedness of the world we find ourselves facing: "a new global economy in which trade, technical development, investment and services form an integrated system."[12]

Approximately one-third of American corporations conduct business abroad, and more than 80 percent of American goods and services compete against foreign sources.[13] As Claire Gaudiani reminds us, most American workers "operate in an increasingly internationalized environment even if they never leave Duluth."[14] America's former preeminence in technological fields and its dominance as a source and destination of capital have come under sustained challenge. Increasingly, our markets, our sources of supply, and our manufacturing have moved offshore.

We watch the radical transformation of traditional trading partners (will it be Fortress Europe or Opportunity Europe?) and the dawning of "the Pacific Century" with hopeful concern: hopeful because in these regions—not to mention Latin America, the former Eastern Bloc, and other areas of the world—we see emerging opportunities; concern because we sense that we may lack the human capital to take advantage of them.

International competitiveness provides a significant rationale for internationalization, but it also has limitations. The very notion of international competition—traditionally embodied in the ideal of home-grown champions operating profitably abroad—may be losing its meaning. The dissociation of businesses from their home countries is increasingly common as domestic enterprises evolve into international, then multinational, then global ones.[15] Economies all over the world tend increasingly to thrive or suffer in concert.[16] This homogenization of enterprises and economies can be seen—perversely, perhaps—as evidence that some aspects of international education are of little real importance.

Increasingly, U.S. businesses value an understanding of other cultures. Since English is the *lingua franca* of international business, however, they tend to put a low priority on developing foreign language skills among their employees; increasingly, they can assume that the latter will be able to conduct business abroad in their native tongue. Any residual need for speakers of a foreign language, say many business leaders, can be "managed"; language proficiency can be bought like any other service from foreign nationals.[17] In any case, alarms about competitiveness notwith-

Some view with suspicion or outright alarm
attempts to involve the university too directly
in any external agenda—perhaps especially one
so closely tied to business and industry

---

standing, few U.S. businesses have so far joined government and private
foundations in supporting international education financially.

There are others for whom arguments based on economic grounds are
problematic. Outside of business schools, particularly, many faculty members are uninterested in manufacturing and balances of trade and regard
these matters as irrelevant to their work.[18] Indeed, some view with suspicion or outright alarm attempts to involve the university too directly in
any external agenda—perhaps especially one so closely tied to business
and industry. Finally, there are those who point out that economic competitiveness is too narrow a formulation even of the national interest, for it
excludes other dimensions of our relations with foreign countries and their
peoples and the acute worldwide need for more *cooperation* in the solution
of common problems.[19]

The fundamental rationale for international education must arise not
from forces external to the university but from our understanding of the
aims of education itself. Our species has been described as biologically and
culturally adapted to the near-at-hand,[20] and overcoming parochialism,
broadly understood, always has been one appropriate goal of schooling. To
be educated is to have a general knowledge of the larger world, some understanding of the array of individual cultures that constitute it, their interdependence, and the place of one's own culture among them. It is to have
some sense of "the complexities of religion and ethnicity, the nuance of
power, and the forces at work in the long, complicated histories of many
nations."[21] It entails, by some definitions, having deeper knowledge and
understanding of at least one foreign culture, including the skills to negoti-
ate the challenges of life there as a speaker of its native tongue. At another level, education is a matter of attitudes and habits of mind—including
those of valuing other cultures and their distinctiveness and seeing things
from the perspective of peoples other than one's own.

The case for international education, however, is only partly that it
serves to produce such directly "international" outcomes. It rests as well
on the special capacity of international education to foster other desirable
qualities—and kinds of learning.

International education helps undermine received opinions of all
types. It can be unsettling and challenging. At its best, however, it fosters
personal growth through reflection on one's assumptions, values, and
moral choices. It challenges students to confront the relativity of things,
but also to make their own grounded judgments. It is active and experien-

tial, putting a premium on competence—on putting what one has learned into effective practice. It accommodates work and service. There may be no better context in which to learn and appreciate the need for multidisciplinarity—for looking at things comparatively, in context, and in their full complexity.

International education, as Victor Stoltzfus has nicely put it, is good education.[22] This is true for all students, not just specialists-in-training. It is true no less in a school of business or engineering than in a college of arts and sciences. As a rationale for internationalizing our colleges and universities, it will likely endure long after today's economic circumstances have passed into history.

THE CHALLENGES AHEAD

Let us turn now to a brief account of the state of internationalization in U.S. colleges and universities. To understand the progress made and the work still to be accomplished, we will look at several key elements of globally oriented programs and institutions: language study, study abroad, foreign students, and the internationalization of the curriculum. In each area, new life is stirring—but daunting work remains to be done.

Language Study

The hapless record of Americans in learning languages has always been an inviting target for humor. Sixty years ago, H. L. Mencken professed indignation at not meeting a single Parisian who spoke second-year college French. A syndicated columnist of our own day writes of high school students who study French for two years—"just long enough to mispronounce 'bonjour'."[23]

The underperformance of our schools and universities in language instruction is a matter for concern, and it is documented by statistics that show it to be a systemic problem. Only 17 percent of public elementary schools offer any form of language instruction (including simple "exposures"),[24] and barely one-third of all high school students take any.[25] Only 8 percent of U.S. colleges and universities require a foreign language for admission,[26] and fewer than 9 percent of universities require one for graduation;[27] it is thus no surprise that only 9 percent of our undergraduates are in foreign language classes.[28] Those that are typically study only for a year or two; very few ever attain even basic proficiency.[29]

Most colleges and universities have a host of
largely unexplored means at their disposal to
change the culture of monolingualism

Also of concern is the relative inattention of our schools and postsecondary institutions to languages other than French, Spanish, and German. Among the so-called Less-Commonly-Taught Foreign Languages (LCTFL's) are Arabic, Chinese, Japanese, and Russian—arguably among those most important for Americans to know in coming decades. LCTFL's, taken together, account for less than 1 percent of all language enrollments at the K–12 level and between 5 and 8 percent of those in college. French, German, and Spanish, on the other hand, account for 90 to 95 percent of all language enrollments—although these languages are spoken by only 14 percent of the world's population.[30]

Nonetheless, there are reasons to be encouraged about the revitalization of language study in this country: renewed student interest, a new focus on proficiency and language for professional uses, new methods of instruction, and the development of exciting instructional technologies.[31] Between 1986 and 1990, language enrollments at colleges and universities rose by nearly 18 percent overall; the increases were even more dramatic in LCTFL's such as Japanese (95 percent) and Russian (31 percent).[32] Some liberal arts colleges now enroll up to 40 percent of their students in language courses; of these, more than 60 percent take courses beyond the first-year level.[33]

Still, more progress in this area will require systemic solutions, including the introduction of American children to language study in far larger numbers and far earlier in their schooling. When postsecondary institutions phase in language requirements, secondary and primary schools will follow suit. Then colleges and universities will be able to focus on what they do best: helping students move from competency to proficiency.[34]

Most colleges and universities have a host of largely unexplored means at their disposal to change the culture of monolingualism. For example, intensive workshops and summer experiences abroad can help faculty members build on existing bases of language study; if their skills were improved, they could use a foreign language in their research and teaching.

Traditional literature-based language study—unfairly maligned in recent years—has much to contribute to any student's liberal education, but expectations and requirements must be framed in terms of communicative competency. Institutions also should find ways to help students make meaningful use of the language they learn, not only during time abroad, but also in other on-campus studies. "Language intensive options," in which students are encouraged to read and write in a second language as part of their work in the major, are a relatively new—and labor-intensive—development. For advanced students and their professors, experiences like these can consolidate hard-won gains and enrich learning in unexpected ways.

Foreign students represent a poorly utilized resource for language instruction. So do the technologies—satellite links, computer software, interactive video disks—that have now made self-instruction a realistic and popular option.

Few strategies can win language study a central place on campus as effectively as linking it to professional fields of study. Too often thought of as something "owned" by the liberal arts, languages have potential constituencies in fields such as engineering, agriculture, health, business, and education.

What an institution cannot do by itself, it might want to consider undertaking with others. Consortial arrangements have proven successful in providing language instruction to students and faculty members, especially in less widely offered languages.

Study Abroad

The typical American student abroad, it is said, is a white, middle-class female from a highly educated professional family who is studying humanities in Western Europe.[35] Implicit in the characterization are several of the key problems that must be overcome if study abroad is to fulfill its vast potential as a component of international education: notably, the small scale of the enterprise and its lack of diversity in terms of participants, locations, and program types.

Reliable statistics on study abroad are difficult to obtain, but recent data do provide answers to some central questions. First, who studies abroad? One answer is almost no one—less than one-half of 1 percent, in fact, of all students enrolled at the baccalaureate level in any given year.[36] At some colleges and universities, of course, the percentages are far higher. Approximately 16 percent of institutions claim to send at least 10 percent of their students abroad at some time in the latter's undergraduate careers.[37] A few selective private colleges can cite participation rates of up to 90 percent. Nationally, however, the numbers are abysmally low.

Another way of answering the question of who goes abroad is in terms of gender: Female students outnumber males by a margin of about two to one.[38] Still another factor is field of study; students majoring in the liberal

Time spent abroad too often does not entail
a full engagement with the host country's
culture—let alone a true immersion in it

---

arts—excluding math and the sciences—are approximately twice as numerous as those majoring in all other fields.[39] Those who are *not* well represented include males, minorities, science majors, working adults, and professional students. Business majors constitute a large and growing subset (11 percent) of those studying abroad, but students in engineering, education, agriculture, and the health sciences are largely absent.[40]

A second basic question is where U.S. students pursue study abroad. The answer—Europe, principally—has changed little over the years. Nearly 80 percent of students pursuing programs abroad do so on the European continent. Indeed, by one count, far more undergraduates (27 percent) study in the United Kingdom alone than in Asia (5 percent), Africa (1 percent), the Middle East (3 percent), and Latin America (9 percent) combined.[41]

As for program type, more than 80 percent of U.S. study abroad students enroll in programs sponsored by a U.S. institution, as opposed to enrolling directly in a foreign institution. About 70 percent of their programs are of a semester's or summer's duration, virtually all are traditionally academic in nature, and they are completed most often during the junior year. Here too, in short, there is a sameness to study abroad programs, with little variation of the kind that might attract and meet the needs of currently unserved populations.[42]

A series of recent analyses on study abroad—by Barbara Burn and Ralph Smuckler, Crauford Goodwin and Michael Nacht, Richard Lambert and others[43]—confirm and extend this critique. The quality and impact of the experience abroad often is not what it should be. Study abroad is a marginal activity on most campuses—unencouraged, unsupported, unprepared for, and unconnected with students' work after their return. Time spent abroad too often does not entail a full engagement with the host country's culture—let alone a true immersion in it. The academic quality of study abroad is suspect in the eyes of some faculty members, and its contributions to learning—as opposed to attitudes and character—are rarely assessed.[44]

The last decade has seen healthy increases in the number of study abroad programs and in the number of participants.[45] Yet by international standards, the U.S. has far to go. The European Community, for example, has launched project ERASMUS, with the immediate aim of ensuring that 10 percent of EC university students have significant experience in another country.

Colleges and universities wishing to improve study abroad and further boost participation can begin by more effectively disseminating information about available options. They can involve faculty members in the design of new programs—a step that not only can remove opposition but can convert it into support. Students going abroad need good information and academic counseling beginning in, or even prior to, their freshman year. Their ability eventually to cope effectively in a host society and take full academic advantage of their time there will depend on their having taken an intelligent selection of language courses and one or more courses in area studies. Students preparing to go abroad can benefit from an orientation seminar as well.

Many—perhaps most—students who have pursued study abroad have experienced problems of academic reentry on their home campuses. Faculty members often see no connection between what the student has done and what they regard as the student's "real" work at the home institution. They are concerned about the "opportunity cost" that has been paid and give little thought to how the student's presumed learning might now be used or shared. Returning students often report that although their study abroad may have been a personally important—even transformative— experience, they rarely are asked about it or encouraged to reflect on its significance.

Clearly, better integration of study abroad into the academic life of the student and the institution is a priority. One good practice in this area would be reentry seminars in which students returning from different regions can share their experiences and enthusiasm with one another—and, ideally, with other U.S. and international students as well as faculty members. Faculty members should be alert for contributions that returning students might make in the classroom and for assignments that might challenge these students to continue building on their learning abroad. One promising option is developing "language-enriched" tracks for such students in one or two courses so that a newly developed fluency is used to enrich the student's further study, rather than allowed to slip away through disuse.

The beauty of study abroad now—as several observers have pointed out—is that all the world is accessible, and everyone can play.[46] Universities and colleges should broaden the reach of their programs both geographically and in terms of who participates. Initiating programs in the Third World can be difficult. Dramatic linguistic and cultural differences, politi-

Foreign students are only 'weakly linked'
with other elements of internationalization
on U.S. campuses

cal risk, incompatible calendars, the unavailability of housing, and other barriers may need to be overcome. But it often is these same regions that present special opportunities: for service learning, new forms of financing (such as debt-for-study arrangements), and acquiring less commonly taught foreign languages.[47]

As study abroad abandons its Eurocentrism, it also must be more flexible. For example, mainstreaming students into local universities—which we might expect and even insist upon for American students in Europe—clearly is not feasible for most U.S. students in Japan. There and elsewhere in Asia for the foreseeable future, English language programs and elementary language instruction have important roles to play.[48]

Flexibility also is essential in involving new types of students. Traditional academic programs may not be suitable for all students, so different options should be available. Internships, which provide both work experience and compensation, are especially promising vehicles for professional students and those who must finance their own education. Independent study and research projects can be tailored to precise academic needs and fit more easily into highly structured programs such as those in engineering and the sciences.[49] While the duration of study abroad should be lengthened for most students,[50] shorter-term options have a role as well. The optimal length and nature of each program depend on each student's particular circumstances and objectives.

International Students

Students from other countries are a potentially important element in the internationalization of American higher education. Although their numbers are substantial and still growing, for a variety of reasons they are not yet the force they clearly might be for the integration of global perspectives into the work of their host campuses.

The U.S. leads all other countries by far in its enrollment of foreign students, hosting nearly one-third of all students worldwide who study outside their native countries. The 420,000 international students enrolled in U.S. institutions account for about 3 percent of total enrollments here—and constitute a cohort about six times as large as that of Americans studying abroad.[51]

The number of non-U.S. undergraduates has been fairly stable; about 47 percent study at the associate or bachelor's level. Although proportions vary by institutional type—with the highest international enrollments in undergraduate programs at Ph.D.-granting universities and selective liberal arts colleges and the lowest at community colleges—international students account for an average of approximately 2 percent of undergraduate enrollments in this country. During the last decade, most of the growth in the enrollment of international students has occurred at the graduate level;[52] U.S. universities have come to rely on them to fill graduate programs and to serve as teaching and research assistants. About 46 percent of foreign students are enrolled at the graduate level; they account for 26 percent of all Ph.D.s granted—including at least one-half of the degrees in math and the sciences.[53]

These numbers, however, obscure characteristics of the international student population that shape and in some ways limit its potential for assisting the internationalizing of U.S. campuses. One is the numerical dominance of Asians, who constitute nearly 60 percent of the whole. By contrast, Europe—the second most frequent region of origin—accounts for only 13 percent; Latin America, the Middle East, and Africa are home to 10, 7, and 5 percent, respectively.[54] Nine of the top ten countries of origin are in Asia, which—with Europe and North America—is one of the only regions from which the flow of students is increasing.[55]

International students also make characteristic field-of-study choices. In four-year institutions, for example, foreign students in 1991–92 most often chose to pursue degrees in business and management (19 percent), engineering (19 percent), physical and life sciences (10 percent), and mathematics and computer sciences (9 percent). They were commensurately under-represented in the humanities (4 percent) and social sciences (8 percent).[56]

As these and similar statistics suggest (and as Richard Lambert has recently pointed out), foreign students are only "weakly linked" with other elements of internationalization on U.S. campuses. A few may serve as resources for area studies centers. Most, however, can be sure that theirnative language skills will go unused; the majority speak Asian languages—not French, German, and Spanish, the languages most often studied by U.S. undergraduates. Nor are foreign students well represented in courses and programs with international content, where they could make significant contributions. Such offerings, by and large, are outside the tightly structured professional, scientific, and technical curricula in which most international students are enrolled. Finally, it is difficult to link American students going abroad with appropriate international students because so

The curriculum should transcend all nationally
and geographically limited, and limiting, frames
of reference

---

many of the latter come from the "wrong" countries, not the European destinations favored by their American counterparts.[57]

In some of these "problems," of course, are opportunities. Particularly as campuses develop programs of study in the Asian languages and study abroad programs in Asian nations, the international students they already are attracting may become valuable sources of assistance. Over the long term, institutions wishing to internationalize in a coherent and comprehensive way will want not only to expand their overall numbers of international students, but also to draw these students in a more representative fashion from various regions of the world. They will work to interest and engage these students across the entire curriculum and co-curriculum, so that they can become resources for the whole campus.

There are many good sources of information on strategies and mechanisms for recruiting, mainstreaming, and making good use of international students. One particular opportunity is afforded by the burgeoning interest among foreign students in business. In the last three years, this field has surpassed engineering as the major most in demand among undergraduates from other countries (20 percent of whom now choose it).[58] The growing presence of these students in business programs—and in the many liberal arts courses those programs require—is an uncommon resource for those who teach and study in both areas.

Internationalizing the Curriculum

Study abroad, language training, and international students notwithstanding, the heart of the matter is internationalizing the curriculum. Courses in microeconomics, literary criticism, marriage and the family, market research, historiography, botany, environmental science—offerings of the kind that constitute the basic building blocks of students' work in the traditional disciplines—should transcend all nationally and geographically limited, and limiting, frames of reference. In their efforts to build international dimensions into their programs, institutions can and should make better use of interdisciplinary approaches as well.

Because college and university curricula are "given shape and direction within the context of the academic disciplines,"[59] the internationalization of these disciplines represents a central challenge. Of course, different disciplines are variously amenable to questions that are international or global in nature. Some fields—international studies, area studies, peace or world order studies—are specifically devoted to examining these kinds of questions. Other disciplines—geography and anthropology, for example—also are intrinsically international in concern. Still other fields, including archeology, botany, geology, linguistics, zoology, entomology, and a number of comparative specialties in the social sciences and humanities, extend their knowledge bases in direct proportion to their access to new materials and sites.[60]

Concerned as they are with universal principles, highly abstract fields such as physics, mathematics, and computer science are not clearly transnational or global in focus. Yet understanding even in these disciplines advances as their practitioners come into contact with the work of colleagues in other countries.[61] Professional fields such as business, law, and medicine are shaped by developments outside the U.S. as surely as they contribute to them. Virtually every discipline presents its practitioners with reasons and opportunities for engaging with the larger world.

Unfortunately, the academy has not always been hospitable to internationally minded scholars. The sociology of the disciplines traditionally has not afforded international studies or peace or world order studies the status enjoyed by their mainstream counterparts. Some faculty members in more traditional fields regard these explicitly international or global fields as lacking in rigor or prone to ideological bias; they may argue that students should gain their international understanding within the rigorous framework, and by using the conceptual tools, of the traditional disciplines.[62] These same faculty members, paradoxically, often shy away from comparative issues in their own courses. Many feel they lack the necessary skills to do this work or are discouraged by its marginality to what is perceived as "the real work" of their disciplines.

In fact, it is increasingly apparent that discovering the international dimensions of any discipline is centrally important intellectual work. Disciplines are powerful ways of seeing, capable of extraordinary clarity and penetration. Yet, as Kenneth Burk put it, a way of seeing also is a way of not seeing. The disciplines afford views that are, at best, partial—and all the more so to the extent that we limit their inquiries to the study of the near-at-hand. Richard Wood contends that Americans in particular need to understand how much their reliance on American and northern European models of the disciplines has distorted their view of the world.[63]

Overcoming scholarly ethnocentrism means asking new questions and reformulating old ones, collecting data from new and possibly far-flung sources, and generalizing from sufficiently diverse observations. The results

Curricula and disciplines will not change
themselves; it is faculty members who
transform both

can be inconvenient and sobering: One may find that prized conclusions
depend on domestic data and analytical approaches, that assumptions do
not travel, that theories and models lose their explanatory power. Japan's
national industrial policy—designed to manipulate markets and gain dominance for that country's enterprises—plays havoc, for example, with ortho-
dox economic models assuming free and open trade.[64] Caught badly off
guard by the rapid break up of the Soviet bloc several years ago, social scientists—largely ignorant of Eastern European thought and politics and perhaps too optimistic about the replicability of American experience elsewhere—have since had to struggle to comprehend why the market and
social reforms there did not take root and flourish as readily as many pre-
dicted they might.[65] What we don't know can clearly hurt us, prompting
simplistic analysis that compromises the quality and credibility of scholarly
judgment.

Clearly, curricula and disciplines will not change themselves. It is faculty members who transform both—provided they have strong international interests and reasonable support for their efforts. A recent survey of
colleges and universities on the subject of faculty involvement in international education, however, suggests that few faculty members are active
agents. Although nearly two-thirds of all institutions claim increasing faculty
involvement in "overseas activities," only a very small fraction of faculty
members do research involving other countries, and just 3 percent super-
vise students abroad or participate in faculty exchanges. Only one in three
institutions claims that even 10 percent of its courses contain international
materials.[66]

Institutional efforts to motivate more faculty members to activate their
natural curiosity as teachers and researchers about the larger world might
take many forms. Within reason, institutional policies affecting hiring, promotion, and tenure, as well as curriculum, should be revised to remove
disincentives to incorporating international perspectives. Faculty members
taking leave abroad, for example, should not have to forego salary increases or be placed at a disadvantage for promotion and tenure because
they publish at a somewhat slower rate or have peers unsympathetic to
comparative or international scholarship.[67]

More positively, promotion and tenure decisions should be recognized
as opportunities to retain and advance internationally minded faculty members—just as every academic search should be considered an opportunity
to secure new ones. The creation of permanent or visiting positions de-

signed for scholars from other countries, the replacement of faculty members away on Fulbright scholarships or sabbaticals by visiting foreign faculty members, and the use of joint appointments to both traditional departments and area studies programs are other effective strategies.[68]

Curriculum committees can be powerful agents of internationalization. They can review the international dimensions of institutional offerings department by department and course by course. They can question, where appropriate, the absence of international content in existing and proposed courses and challenge faculty members to justify syllabi that focus only on the United States.[69]

Institutions wishing to internationalize the faculty should actively promote faculty and curriculum development. There are many ways of doing this: Faculty members can be encouraged to spend periods of leave in other countries, participate in international development projects and foreign conferences, or to undertake joint research with foreign scholars; sources of funding for study and research abroad can be publicized on campus; faculty members can be offered summer salary and foreign study expenses to develop new internationally oriented courses; release time during the academic year can be provided to faculty members introducing international courses; and, finally, institutions can encourage—as well as train and pay—a wider circle of faculty members to design and lead study abroad programs.

Few strategies have wider impact on a campus than organizing internationally oriented workshops for groups of interested faculty members. These might take the form of seminars on areas or issues, such as sub-Saharan Africa or global hunger; intensive language study; or a combination of two or more of these approaches. Programs of this kind can be especially effective if they are sustained by the institution, involve a period of group travel abroad, and carry an expectation that participants change their courses to reflect what they have learned. Institutions that have minimal faculty turnover may find such workshops an especially helpful way to keep faculty members current and motivated.

A useful variant is the development of workshops or training programs under consortial auspices. This can prove especially practical in the case of less commonly taught languages or areas, or where particular institutions have special resources or interests they can share with faculty members from other colleges and universities, perhaps on a reciprocal basis.

Implementation aside, there is much hard
thinking to be done about purposes

BUSINESS-LIBERAL ARTS FACULTY COLLABORATION

In the past, the major components of international education were viewed
largely as self-contained. Foreign languages and international and area studies were not traditionally seen as having much to do with other disciplines
in the arts and sciences—much less with engineering, law, medicine, or
business. Yet the attitudes and understandings that are the goals of international education cannot be adequately taught in disciplinary enclaves or
separate courses. A strong international education requires carefully
planned and executed interdisciplinary collaboration.[70]

A partnership between business and the liberal arts is one particularly
robust possibility. As each of these domains tries to come to terms with a
world of profoundly integrated issues and problems, each produces helpful
but unintegrated insights and approaches. By integrating their fields of vision, faculty members in these two areas can begin to develop larger and
more adequate structures of understanding. International education is a particular priority in both domains, and it is an area in which business and
liberal arts disciplines have much of value to share with one another.

Not that the marriage comes easily: As Richard Lambert reminds us,
business and liberal arts faculty members are traditionally two hostile
tribes—subcultures with their own definitions of purpose, their own no-
tions of what is worth learning, their own eruditions. In particular, business, as too few in the liberal arts understand, is oriented to decision-
making and employs an intellectual approach—cost-benefit analysis—that
for students tends to be the dominant gene in the hybrid.[71]

Yet the effort to draw the two together must be made. The benefits
are many and mutual. International business, for example, raises for arts
and sciences students many social, economic, political, and ethical issues
central to their work in the disciplines. Good case studies challenge these
students to test their theoretical understandings against the messy realities
of real-world situations. International business internships offer especially
helpful opportunities for arts and sciences students to apply language skills
in practical settings.

Business students, for their part, stand to develop a better appreciation for complexity, context, and ambiguity in a course of study that com-
bines business and liberal arts perspectives. A well-known case study
demanding a decision on investment in a Philippines silver mine, for
example, encourages students to be more thoughtful about political risk.
Another—on the disastrous introduction of a new light beer into

Mexico—helps students understand connections between and among cultural difference, semiotics, and product marketing. Through their work in the liberal arts, business students may even learn a second language—and be able to use it advantageously both as a means of communicating and as a window to another culture.

Of course, these examples could be multiplied and extended to research and service, as well as instruction. The point is clear, however: The disciplines of business and the liberal arts can and should look to each other for new frameworks, strategies of inquiry, and modes of learning. They will find one another especially relevant as they both seek a global perspective.[72]

CONCLUSION

It has been said of colleges and universities that their besetting vice is to turn inward.[73] On the other hand, Manuel Pachecho and Celestino Fernandez are equally correct in saying that these institutions have a "natural and historical inclination toward a global perspective."[74] The foregoing discussion suggests where those wishing to realize such a perspective in their own institutions can begin working.

We use the word "work" advisedly. Implementation aside, there is much hard thinking to be done, for instance, about purposes. Is the particular institution or program aspiring to ensure awareness of international differences, understanding of such differences, or real competence in actually negotiating them? Different approaches and different levels of resources are implied by each goal. Difficult as achieving agreement may be, it is essential to knowing one's course.[75]

Once purposes are clarified, there is the difficult task of thinking comprehensively about elements that we have had the luxury here of discussing in sequential fashion. Perhaps every major should have language and study abroad options—and possibly the option of an international concentration, as well. Perhaps, however, since no institution can be all things to all people, what is needed is a strategy of selective excellence that reinforces certain areas of prior strength. Then again, there is the desideratum of balance—an approach that appropriately internationalizes both general education and the major, gives basic attention to all world regions, leaves no discipline entirely untouched, and attends adequately to both international and, more properly, global issues.[76]

The college or university willing to undertake a vigorous process of assessment, planning, and reorientation will do much to position itself for the future. We hope that the pages preceding and following help as many institutions as possible to accomplish that important goal.

1. Sven Groennings, "Higher Education, International Education and the Academic Disciplines" in *Group Portrait: Internationalizing the Disciplines*, Sven Groennings and David S. Wiley, eds. (New York: The American Forum, 1990), 28.

2. Thomas C. Heller, quoted in Edward B. Fiske, "The Global Imperative," *New York Times Education Supplement*, 9 April 1989, 19; Richard Lambert, *International Studies and the Undergraduate* (Washington, D.C.: American Council on Education, 1989), 1.

3. Groennings, *Group Portrait*, 16–17; Crauford D. Goodwin and Michael Nacht, *Missing the Boat: The Failure to Internationalize American Higher Education* (Cambridge: University Press, 1991), 3–4 and 110–111.

4. Sarah M. Pickert, *Preparing for a Global Community: Achieving an International Perspective in Higher Education*, ASHE-ERIC Higher Education Report No. 2. (Washington, D.C.: The George Washington University, 1992), 5.

5. Goodwin and Nacht, *Missing the Boat*, 112.

6. Pickert, *Preparing for a Global Community*, 6.

7. Association of International Education Administrators Task Force on International and Economic Competitiveness, "Educating Americans for Tomorrow's World," quoted in Burkart Holzner, "Economic Competitiveness and International Education," *National Forum* 68 (Fall 1988): 12.

8. Ibid., 6–7.

9. Groennings, *Group Portrait*, 29.

10. Goodwin and Nacht, *Missing the Boat*, 114.

11. David P. Gardner, "Internationalization: The State of the Institution," *Educational Record* 71 (Spring 1990): 9.

12. Preamble to Omnibus Trade and Competitiveness Act of 1988.

13. Commission on International Education, "What We Can't Say Can Hurt Us" (revised draft, April 17, 1989), 2.

14. Claire Gaudiani quoted in Fiske, "The Global Imperative," 18.

15. Gary Clyde Hufbauer, "Europe 1992: Opportunities and Challenges," *The Brookings Review* 8 (Summer 1990): 21–22.

16. David Wessel, "World's Economies, Now Interdependent, All Suffer Together," *The Wall Street Journal*, 17 September 1992.

17. Carol S. Fixman, "The Foreign Language Needs of U.S.-Based Corporations," National Foreign Language Center Occasional Paper 5, May 1989, 1–17.

18. Rose C. Hayden and Kurt E. Muller, Preface to Groennings, *Group Portrait*, ix.

19. Sarah Pickert and Barbara Turlington, *Internationalizing the Undergraduate Curriculum: A Handbook for Campus Leaders* (Washington: American Council on Education, 1992), 105.

20. Tom McConaghy, "Global Education: Learning to Think in a New Way," *Phi Delta Kappan* (April 1990): 646–648.

21. Parker G. Marden and David C. Engerman, "In the International Interest: Liberal Arts Colleges Take the High Road," *Educational Record* (Spring 1992): 42.

22. Victor Stoltzfus, presentation to International 50 meeting, Beloit, Wisconsin, 1992.

23. James J. Kilpatrick, "Illiterates Abroad: Our Neglect of Foreign Languages Must End," *Annapolis Capital,* October 10, 1991, 10.

24. Commission on International Education, "What We Can't Say," 8.

25. Kilpatrick, "Illiterates Abroad," 10.

26. Gardner, "Internationalization," 10.

27. Commission on International Education, "What We Can't Say," 8.

28. Marden and Engerman, "In the International Interest," 43.

29. Pickert, *Preparing for a Global Community,* 13.

30. A. Ronald Walton, "Expanding the Vision of Foreign Language Education: Enter the Less Commonly Taught Languages," National Foreign Language Center Occasional Paper 10, February 1992, 1–7.

31. See Groennings, *Group Portrait,* 20.

32. National Endowment for the Humanities unpublished report for the National Security Education Program, Table 10, March 1992.

33. Parker G. Marden and David C. Engerman, *In the International Interest: The Contributions and Needs of America's International Liberal Arts Colleges* (Beloit, Wisconsin: International Liberal Arts Colleges, 1992), 40.

34. Henry R. Cooper, Jr., "Foreign Language and Today's Interdependent World," *National Forum* 68 (Fall 1988): 16.

35. Council on International Educational Exchange quoted in Fiske, "The Global Imperative," 19.

36. Commission on International Education, "What We Can't Say", 2.

37. Elaine El–Khawas, *Campus Trends, 1992,* Higher Education Panel Report 82, American Council on Education, July 1992, 13.

38. Advisory Council for International Educational Exchange, *Educating for Global Competence* (New York: Council on International Educational Exchange, 1988), 25.

39. National Endowment for the Humanities, unpublished report, Table 3.

40. Ibid. See also Advisory Council for International Exchange, *Educating for Global Competence,* 7–10.

41. National Endowment for the Humanities, unpublished report, Tables 1 and 2; National Task Force on Undergraduate Education Abroad, *A National Mandate for Education Abroad* (Washington: NAFSA, 1990), 6.

42. Ibid., 8; National Endowment for the Humanities, unpublished report, Tables 6, 5, and 4.

43. See National Task Force on Undergraduate Education Abroad, *A National Mandate;* Crauford D. Goodwin and Michael Nacht, *Abroad and Beyond: Patterns in American Overseas Education* (Cambridge: Cambridge University Press, 1988); and Richard D. Lambert, *International Studies and the Undergraduate* (Washington, D.C.: American Council on Education, 1989).

44. Lambert, *International Studies,* 36–41.

45. Ibid., 10; Goodwin and Nacht, *Abroad and Beyond,* 1.

46. Goodwin and Nacht, *Abroad and Beyond,* 118.

47. National Task Force on Undergraduate Education Abroad, *A National Mandate,* 6–8.

48. Ibid., 11.

49. Ibid., 7–8.

50. Lambert, *International Studies*, 161.

51. Marianthi Zikopoulos, ed., *Open Doors 1991/92: Report on International Educational Exchange* (New York: Institute of International Education, 1992), 1–13.

52. Richard D. Lambert, "International Challenges for American Higher Education: Student Flows and the Internationalization of Higher Education," paper presented at the meeting of the Consortium on Financing Higher Education, Cambridge, Massachusetts, October 4–5, 1992, 26–31.

53. Anthony DePalma, "Foreigners Flood U.S. Graduate Schools," *New York Times*, November 29, 1990.

54. Zikopoulos, ed., *Open Doors*, 15.

55. Ibid., 7, 14.

56. Ibid., 30.

57. Lambert, *International Challenges*, 52–53.

58. Zikopoulos, ed., *Open Doors*, 25.

59. Groennings, *Group Portrait*, 2.

60. Ibid., 22; Richard D. Lambert. *Points of Leverage: An Agenda for a National Foundation for International Studies* (New York: Social Science Research Council, 1986), 125.

61. Ibid., 125–126.

62. Jaroslav Pelikan, "Essential Embrace," *Yale* (March 1992): 33; Groennings, *Group Portrait*, 27.

63. Richard Wood, "Toward Cultural Empathy: A Framework for Global Education," *Educational Review*, Fall 1991, 10.

64. Kevin L. Kearns, "The Economic Orthodoxies Offered U.S. Students Won't Prepare Them to Work in World Markets," *Chronicle of Higher Education*, March 27, 1991, B1–3.

65. Stjepan G. Metrovic, "Point of View," *Chronicle of Higher Education*, September 25, 1991, A56.

66. El-Khawas, *Campus Trends*, 1992, 12–14.

67. Humphrey Tonkin and Jane Edwards, "Internationalizing the University: The Arduous Road to Euphoria," *Educational Record*, Spring 1990, 14–17.

68. See George C. Christensen, *International Curriculum for the Professions, National Forum*, Fall 1988, 27–30.

69. Tonkin and Edwards, "Internationalizing the University," 16.

70. Commission on International Education, *What We Don't Know Can Hurt Us: The Shortfall in International Competence* (Washington, D.C.: American Council on Education, n.d.), 14. See also, Maurice Harari, "Internationalization of Higher Education," Report No. 1, *Occasional Report Series on the Internationalization of Higher Education*, Center for International Education, California State University, Long Beach, 1989.

71. Richard Lambert, "Business Education and Liberal Arts," Unpublished remarks at conference, sponsored by Association of American Colleges and American Assembly of Collegiate Schools of Business, Lincolnshire, Illinois, March 27, 1991.

72. Groennings, *Group Portrait*, 29.

73. Pelikan, "Essential Embrace," 31.

74. Manuel Pachecho and Celestino Fernandez, "Knowing No Boundaries: The University as World Citizen," *International Record*, Spring 1992, 23.

75. See Jeffrey Arpan, "Internationalization: Curricular and Structural Considerations—The Cheshire Cat Parable," unpublished remarks presented at Michigan State University Round-table on Internationalizing Business Schools and Faculty, East Lansing, Michigan, June 6–7, 1991.
76. Lambert, *International Studies*, 165–6.

PROFILES IN INTERNATIONAL EDUCATION

BABSON COLLEGE

What do business law, world politics, and speech communications have in common? They are all part of a complex and intellectually challenging course cluster that provides students at Babson College with an integrated, multidisciplinary learning experience.

Supported by a grant from the National Endowment for the Humanities, Babson has been experimenting since 1985 with the "cluster course" approach—an innovative strategy for integrating curricular material and knowledge from two or more distinct courses while maintaining the integrity of the disciplines. Each course cluster has the following elements: it has two or more courses that are linked by a set of common themes or issues; faculty members must agree to plan their courses together—sharing some common texts, assignments, lectures, and, most important, students; faculty members must meet periodically during the semester to discuss student progress, teaching, and learning development; and the pedagogical approach must be coordinated to ensure that students integrate not only course content but skills development in writing, oral presentations, and small-group work.

A cluster course involves neither team teaching nor the segmentation of a course into separate parts. Each faculty member teaching in the cluster retains the disciplinary focus of his or her own course; together, the instructors in each cluster agree to coordinate themes or issues across courses in the cluster. The cluster approach avoids difficulties frequently associated with team-taught courses about who teaches what and who is in charge of problems. It also demands intellectual creativity and requires students and faculty members to integrate ideas, concepts, and skills across disciplinary boundaries. An accounting professor must pay attention to students' writing skills, for example, while a colleague in literature must understand and teach the ways in which a novel or a play conveys cultural circumstances that affect business/management values and decisions.

Cluster courses also can have disadvantages. They are expensive, since lower student-faculty ratios are desirable as both an incentive for faculty members to take the extra planning time required and a pedagogical necessity given the need to focus on the ability of students to integrate learning experiences. Clusters can be difficult to develop at the junior and senior levels—although such efforts are underway—where specialized knowledge and advanced disciplinary understanding are more important than at the freshman and sophomore levels. Finally, clusters are intellectually and pedagogically challenging—so faculty commitment and interest are critical variables.

Examples of clusters abound at Babson: Chinese history and marketing in Asia; international law and modern drama; ethics and advanced economics. "Many international topics lend themselves to multidisciplinary intellectual frameworks," says Carolyn Hotchkiss, professor of business law—and thus are ideal for building a cluster. Culture, history, and political economy are all useful in explaining patterns of international trade, for example. One element that holds the clusters together appears to be a general commitment to emphasizing small-group writing and oral presentation skills. This helps provide a common language and assignments, as well as evaluations of student performance and compatible classroom formats.

Babson's success derives from a number of factors, according to Kelly Lynch, director of the cluster program. The cluster approach was implemented gradually over a period of years. Faculty members were involved in its development from the beginning; indeed, it was faculty-conceived, not mandated by the administration. Babson also has a more flexible organizational structure than many institutions. Its small size and sense of institutional mission seem to dominate over disciplinary and departmental loyalties.

Moreover, one of the major themes that defines the philosophy of educators at Babson is the desire to integrate international and global perspectives across the curriculum. This gave a boost to the cluster approach; faculty members and students see the cluster concept as a resource in implementing that philosophy. Finally, Babson's policy in hiring, tenure, and promotion matters is to stimulate and reward cross-disciplinary teaching and pedagogical experimentation. New hires are expected to be prepared to teach in clusters; faculty evaluations recognize teaching in clusters as a sign of teaching ability and intellectual rigor.

Hotchkiss notes that many faculty members have international interests and backgrounds. Babson also has a large international student population, which has helped to develop an ethos of multiculturalism.

A design for Babson's efforts to internationalize was provided by a strategic plan adopted in 1989 after an extensive campuswide planning process that involved senior administrators and more than thirty faculty members. Objectives and missions are clearer, faculty resources better used, and student quality higher, says Hotchkiss. In this context, the cluster course model promises to continue playing an important role in creating an active, stimulating, and internationally oriented learning environment.

BENTLEY COLLEGE

When the leaders of Bentley College decided in 1986 to develop international education, they started with the faculty. A business school—albeit one with a history of strong programs in the liberal arts—Bentley had relatively few faculty members with significant international experience.

Today, more than a quarter of the 208 full-time faculty members have been directly involved in the college's multi-faceted international program. They take part in faculty development seminars, funded exchange programs, foreign study, and travel with Bentley students. They are under contract to teach groups of foreign students on the Bentley campus and consult with institutions of higher education abroad. According to Jerome Bookin-Weiner, executive director of international programs, faculty involvement now also cuts across all departments, including some—such as accounting and computer information systems—that might have been considered among the most resistant to international education.

Bentley, an institution of approximately 3,400 full-time undergraduates and 2,200 graduate students, has raised funds aggressively for its new international emphasis. This money supports the college's strengths as an American business school with expertise of potential interest to institutions abroad. For example, Bentley has secured two grants from the U.S. Department of Education for curriculum and faculty development, as well as outreach to businesses and secondary education. The United States Information Agency (USIA) has funded two faculty exchange programs—one with Yunnan University in China and one with the Estonian Management Institute in Tallinn, Estonia, in which Bentley faculty members train and serve as consultants to their Estonian counterparts at all of that Baltic republic's faculties of economics. A third exchange, supported by the binational U.S.-Egyptian Fulbright Commission, links Bentley with the Sadat Academy of Management Sciences in Cairo. A fourth, with the Ateneo de Manila University in the Philippines, is supported by a federal grant un-

Faculty members who four or five years ago
were skeptical about the international emphasis
now accept it as one of the institution's areas
of distinctive strength

---

der which Bentley—in partnership with the Fletcher School of Law and
Diplomacy at Tufts University—has served as a Center for International
Business Education and Research (CIBER). Another USIA grant is funding
an extensive eighteen-month program to refocus and upgrade the faculty
and curriculum of the Faculty of Economics at the University of Tartu in
Estonia.

Even this list of grants does not convey the extent of Bentley's international entrepreneurism. The college has agreements with institutions in
Brussels, Melbourne, Puebla (Mexico), and Paris that enable its undergraduate business majors to study abroad for an academic year or semester.
There also are summer programs in Strasbourg, Tokyo, Cambridge, and
Hong Kong/ Kunming, China. The college has tailored programs on its
own campus for students from partner institutions in Japan, Armenia, Italy, and Spain. It is helping an institution in Barcelona design and launch
an American-style business school. To provide an even more extensive network for faculty exchange and cooperative projects, Bentley has taken the
lead in setting up the new International Consortium for Business and Management Education—which counts among its other members institutions
in the United States, France, Spain, Belgium, Estonia, Egypt, Mexico,
Brazil, Australia, and New Zealand.

One of Bentley's most recent grants is supporting the development of
core courses for a new undergraduate major in international culture and
economy. This support has come through a grants competition jointly administered by the Association of American Colleges and the American Assembly of Collegiate Schools of Business and funded by the KPMG Peat
Marwick Foundation.

Much remains to be accomplished at Bentley, according to Bookin-
Weiner. The MBA program is being internationalized through the introduction of graduate study tours and a revised MBA core focusing on the global
aspects of business. The development of foreign internships also is a priority. Some think that the B.S. degree program in business should, like the
minor in international business, require language study.

Bentley's initiatives in fundraising, in establishing inter-institutional
ties, and in faculty and curriculum development already have changed the
learning environment at the college, as well as the attitudes and aspirations of those who study and teach there. The college has a more international flavor today, Bookin-Weiner says. Language courses focus more

aggressively on developing oral proficiency, and courses in other disciplines incorporate newly developed international modules. Faculty members who four or five years ago were skeptical about the international emphasis now accept it as one of the institution's areas of distinctive strength. Moreover, despite the New England region's economic downturn, Bentley has managed to increase the number of its undergraduates taking advantage of the opportunity to study abroad.

Bentley students who go abroad tend to be the ones most profoundly changed by the new emphasis, Bookin-Weiner says. Business students often go to college primarily for the technical skills that will secure them a job, he notes; few have developed any interest in service and culture. "When they go, say, to Belgium and are expected to take a course in the cultural history of Europe and to visit museums, cathedrals, and other cultural sites, they may resist," Bookin-Weiner says. "But, of course, they go—and by the end of their semester abroad they are changed. There are several weeks at the end of the term abroad during which students are encouraged to pursue their interests independently. These same students—the business majors—end up using that time to visit museums and cathedrals on their own."

BOSTON COLLEGE

The story of the European Perspectives Program (EPP) at Boston College is a tale of how a university with historical roots as a regional, urban, Jesuit college stretched its vision to include not only a national mission but an international dimension.

Before EPP was initiated in 1992, Boston College had never tried to develop a cross-disciplinary program or course between two graduate schools. Yet what started out as the development of a program on contemporary European business and culture ended up providing a timely opportunity to develop an exchange with a French business school, a network of alumni and corporate contacts in France, and, most importantly, a vehicle for pedagogical and organizational experimentation.

EPP is a three-week cultural immersion experience in France that focuses on the impact of European integration on management culture and business practices. Following a semester-long orientation seminar, eighteen graduate students from BC's business school and college of arts and science travel to France in May with a team of three faculty members (two from business and one from romance languages). Ten days are spent in Paris,

Adopting a more international focus was easy
to justify, but the practical tasks of finding
resources and developing mechanisms to
implement changes were less straightforward

---

where site visits to firms are organized around a series of seminars on European integration. This is followed by a second ten-day module at the École Supérieure de Commerce de Clermont-Ferrand, a business school in the Auvergne region. There, students are paired with French counterparts and work on a series of case studies of French and European firms. The case analyses and discussions are led by faculty members from the French and American institutions. Students from both countries study and live together during the program.

What makes the EPP experience unusual is its interdisciplinary character and its link to an institutional effort to increase interaction among graduate school faculty members and students from different fields. According to Marian St. Onge, the campus director of international programs, EPP represents BC's first attempt to encourage graduate-level interdisciplinary teaching with an international theme.

Recognizing the need to consider new ways of organizing graduate studies—which stressed disciplinary specialization—BC's academic vice president first instituted an effort to increase opportunities for collaboration in teaching and scholarship across disciplinary lines. EPP is one element of this larger initiative. The creation of an Office of International Programs to develop and encourage international curricula and programs provided the stimulus for the development of the program.

St. Onge's appointment as the first director of international programs came with a mandate and resources to develop new activities. An advisory committee of respected faculty members and deans from across the campus supported the effort by considering how international activities fit into the larger mission of the college. Boston College's Jesuit identity provided some guidance: Since international exchange and travel were long traditions in the Jesuit order, extending the teaching and research activities beyond the regional or national focus of the past seemed logical.

Adopting a more international focus was easy to justify, but the practical tasks of finding resources and developing mechanisms to implement changes were less straightforward. St. Onge knew that she had to capture the interest and imagination of the faculty to be successful in developing new activities and programs. She recognized the interdisciplinary nature of most international scholarship and teaching and realized that pedagogical approaches would have to be different than in the past.

The proposal to develop EPP came out of discussions with colleagues in the arts and sciences as well as faculty members in the business school.

Acceptance of the idea of creating a cross-disciplinary program at the graduate level was not a foregone conclusion. There was a great deal of skepticism on the part of faculty members regarding the value of a summer immersion program in another country. They had to be convinced that the program would have the rigor and coherence of the regular graduate curriculum. Agreement was easier to achieve at the undergraduate level, where there was less specialization and greater flexibility in the requirements. Yet the real test of the value attached to a stronger international mission for the institution was the capacity to integrate international programs into graduate study and to encourage options and opportunities for cross-disciplinary collaboration.

To achieve her objective, St. Onge first gained the support of deans in the schools of business and the arts and sciences and invited top-flight faculty members to teach in the program. It was "hard to get them to commit to a broader vision beyond their own departments," she says, "but the program needed to be the result of our own development efforts to which we were all committed." After a proposal was developed, financial commitments from the campus administration were obtained and efforts were undertaken to obtain outside funding.

A small grant was obtained from the matching grants program sponsored by the KPMG Peat Marwick Foundation and administered by AAC and AACSB. According to St. Onge, the additional money was less important than the legitimacy conferred by receiving external validation of the value of this project. Students selected to the program were named "Peat Marwick Fellows" and received publicity and attention from campus media and the local press. The symbolic value of receiving the grant far outweighed any financial benefit, St. Onge says.

Even with faculty support and adequate funding, the task of organizing the program was not easy. Faculty members had to work together to develop a syllabus for the semester-long orientation course (including an option to study "survival French"), and negotiations had to be undertaken with the French partner institution jointly to design the "immersion" in European business and culture. Finally, links with business firms in France needed to be established to ensure site visits and contact with managers.

The faculty team that worked on the project developed networks of alumni, foreign colleagues, and company representatives that ultimately enabled them to offer a well-integrated program. The latter included visits to companies, a multidisciplinary lecture series, case-study analyses by teams of French and American students, and a cultural program in Paris and Clermont-Ferrand. In the summer of 1994, a group of students and faculty members from the École Supérieure de Clermont-Ferrand will come to Boston for a reciprocal experience focusing on American business and culture.

Curricular and pedagogical innovations and the development of an international partnership are among EPP's contributions to Boston College. The program's success, conversely, appears to derive from a high level of faculty involvement and commitment, support from deans and the academic vice chancellor, and a consonance with a larger campus objective of increasing cross-disciplinary activity at the graduate level.

COLLEGE OF STATEN ISLAND, CITY UNIVERSITY OF NEW YORK

Cultura e Commercio. Culture et Commerce. Cultura y Comercio. By any of its several names, the Culture and Commerce program at the College of Staten Island (CSI) of the City University of New York is noteworthy for its combination of undergraduate study in the liberal arts and business and for its emphasis on experiential education. It also exemplifies a particularly effective use of a college's location—in this case, proximity to the international center that is Manhattan and immediate location in the predominately ethnic borough of Staten Island.

Culture and Commerce is a four-year course of study, equivalent in length to a very substantial academic minor. It allows students majoring in the arts and sciences to develop fluency in Italian, French, or Spanish; complete a sequence of courses in international business; spend a semester studying abroad; and complete a semester's internship—typically, in the New York office of an international business. It also offers students opportunities to receive special advising and to participate in social and cultural activities that bring them together with the program's friends and patrons from the local and professional communities.

The program was begun in 1988 by the Dean of Humanities and Social Sciences, Mirella Affron, and faculty colleagues in the foreign languages and in the international business section of the college's business department. Affron believed that the key to reversing enrollment declines in the college's language departments was to convince students, especially nonmajors, that there are practical uses for the languages taught there. To do this, she and her colleagues decided to develop both study-abroad and career-related internship options.

They faced several challenges. CSI students are mostly from the local area and locally-oriented; many lack the resources to think seriously about traditional study abroad. There were no college funds to support foreign study, and the college had few ties with firms that might provide internship placements.

Recognizing that a majority of Staten Island residents, including most of its business and professional community, are of Italian descent, the college launched the Commerce and Culture program with a focus on Italy. It organized partnerships with local businesses, organizations, and individuals that might support a new international program with this focus. When Karen Masters-Wicks joined the college as the program's coordinator in 1990, she brought with her Manhattan business contacts that have proved helpful in providing the program with internships.

The college's relationships with the program's friends and patrons have been developed carefully, and on several occasions, special cultural activities have been organized to involve the latter. In one instance, the program purchased one hundred tickets for a performance of La Bohème at the City Opera, then resold them to students, faculty members, and local supporters to benefit the program's scholarship fund. In a special preparatory seminar for ticket holders, Affron provided background on La Bohème, and Masters, an accomplished opera singer, performed selections. Other recent cultural events and fundraisers included a performance by a dance troupe from Galicia, Spain and a wine-and-cheese party cosponsored by the Italian Trade Commission to introduce new Italian vintages.

While putting the off-campus components of the program in place, the original planning group also devised an extensive on-campus curriculum that builds on pre-existing offerings in modern language, business, and the social sciences. The group designed the curriculum for the broadest possible range of students. Participants need not have previously studied a foreign language, and they may be enrolled in any of a large number of majors within the arts and sciences (although preferably an applicable foreign language or International Studies).

Once enrolled in the program, students take eight to twelve credits in the foreign language of their choice at CSI and then up to twelve more credits during their semester abroad. Before, during, or after this semester—which usually occurs in the junior year—they also take one or more courses in the history of civilization of the country or countries in which their chosen language is spoken. The professional component of the pro-

CSI students value the program's internships as opportunities for testing their career interests and the applicability of their academic preparation, as well as for acquiring international work experience

gram is a six-course sequence which includes one course each in computing and economics, an introductory business course, and three courses in international business. With an emphasis on political, economic, technological, and cultural influences, the international business courses explore how financial, marketing, and other management decisions are made in an international context.

A crucial three-year grant from the Fund for Improvement of Postsecondary Education (FIPSE) helped launch the program, and external support from the program's patrons has sustained it. An advisory committee of language and business faculty still oversees the program, which is administered by Masters-Wicks and a part-time secretary. This small central staff plans cultural and fundraising events and administers a club to promote community among the students and faculty in the program.

Masters-Wicks also advises all Commerce and Culture students. The largest part of her time, however, is spent developing internship placements. Study-abroad sites—universities in Seville, Spain; Florence, Italy; Aix-en-Provence, France; and Guayaquil, Ecuador—are the same for most students, but internships are carefully designed to fit the student's academic background, language skills, and career interests.

This tailoring of internships is as distinctive and important a feature of the program as its aggressive outreach to neighboring employers—and, of course, a principal reason for it. According to Masters-Wicks, many of CSI's students not only lack international exposure, they have little sense of what the working world here or abroad is like and often do not understand how their skills might be used. The program has viewed these circumstances as an opportunity for its internships to serve several needs at once. An English major might be placed in the publishing office or the archival division of the Italian Cultural Institute; students majoring in political science might be placed in law firms where the language they have studied is widely used. CSI students therefore value the program's internships as opportunities for testing their career interests and the applicability of their academic preparation, as well as for acquiring international work experience.

The program currently enrolls seventy students; since it is only six years old, it has had only a handful of graduates. Assessment is still in the future, but those who oversee the program say that it clearly influences students—both in their immediate career directions and their larger aspirations and growth. One of the first graduates, for example, already is working in an international capacity for the Rolex Corporation in New York. Another, an English major, cannot be found for comment; after doing a successful internship at NCZ, New York City's Italian language radio station, he left to set up his own company—in Italy.

EASTERN MICHIGAN UNIVERSITY

Like several of the institutions described here, Eastern Michigan University (EMU) began to build its international offerings in response to a crisis. Two of the programs that resulted are distinctive: a now widely replicated program in language and international trade and a permanent mechanism to foster an international dimension across the campus, EMU's World College.

For several years in the early 1970s, few if any graduates of EMU's language department were able to find jobs. A weak economy and demographic shifts had conspired to severely reduce the number of openings for elementary and secondary teachers—a very unhappy development for this institution of 26,000 students that has traditionally certified more teachers than any other institution in the state. As teaching and other career prospects diminished, foreign language enrollments plummeted; the number of majors declined by 90 percent. By 1975, the situation was so worrisome that a gubernatorially appointed commission recommended closing the university's language department.

The recommendation was never implemented, but it and the enrollment drops caught the attention of the faculty. These factors also strengthened the hands of critics who believed that the curriculum was outmoded and left those who were resistant to change few credible reasons for being so. By the late 1970s, a proposal for a new program—Language and International Trade—had been drawn up, approved, and implemented on both the graduate and undergraduate levels, and enrollments had begun a strong recovery. By the mid-1980s, the program had more than three hundred graduate and undergraduate majors—compared to a previous peak, in the post-Sputnik era, of approximately 150.

The new Language and International Trade program originally offered tracks in French, Spanish, and German. An option in Japanese, added in 1986, also is now well-enrolled. Chinese and Arabic are offered as well—although classes in these languages are staffed through the Office of Continuing Education.

One of the best features of the World College
is that it has no traditional academic or
political 'turf'

Based in the College of Arts and Sciences, the undergraduate Language and International Trade program entails fifty-seven semester hours of coursework and a practical training assignment. In addition to a minimum of eighteen hours of language study—which includes courses at the 300 and 400 levels—students take thirty hours in business and economics. The business portion of the curriculum consists of twenty-one to twenty-four hours, in an operational area of the student's choosing (such as marketing or finance), and three hours in international business. The economics portion includes macro- and microeconomics and a course in either comparative economic systems or international economics. Students also complete six hours of study of the history and geography of the regions in which their chosen languages are spoken, and take one of numerous internationally focused political science offerings.

The program offers international field experiences for students (both graduate and undergraduate) wishing to participate in a cooperative work exchange in an area of the world where the language they have studied is spoken. In 1978 EMU created the International Cooperative Education Exchange (ICEE) to foster agreements between U.S. and foreign institutions willing to make reciprocal student placements. Since that time, the ICEE program has placed three hundred U.S. and foreign students—including many from EMU's Language and International Trade program. Students have earned both pay and academic credit for three- to twelve-month practical training assignments outside of their home country. They have undertaken internships with (among other firms) Renault and ELF-Aquitaine in France, PROSENA and INTELSA in Spain, and Daimler-Benz, Siemens, Bosch, and Volkswagen in Germany.

That success breeds success is borne out by what happened next at Eastern Michigan. In 1985, the state of Michigan reviewed the accomplishments of the Language and International Trade program and the ICEE and decided that it would be in the state's interest to increase its investment in these kinds of programs. That year, EMU received an allocation of $200,000 to support international initiatives. This grant has been continued with regular increments each year since. This funding supplements the instructional budget for Language and International Trade. With the encouragement of John Porter, the university's president at the time of that first award, academic leaders developed and won approval to use this support and other newly freed-up university funds, to develop a new administrative unit called World College.

As Ray Schaub—a professor of German and the director of the World College—explains, this new entity, launched in 1987, is not a traditional academic unit with its own faculty, curricula, and students. Instead, it is a center of expertise and funding that is put at the service of EMU faculty members interested in developing global perspectives in their teaching and research. For example, Title VI grants raised through the World College have supported the infusion of international content into business courses and led to new work on internationalizing general education. The college also has provided travel funds for faculty members interested in attending international conferences, and it asks faculty following their return to report on their success in developing new international content for their courses.

According to Schaub, one of the best features of the World College is that it has no traditional academic or political "turf." Therefore it is not seen as being in competition with other units. What Schaub and his staff (an associate director, an international placement coordinator, and two secretaries) do have is the freedom and the resources to provide help to interested faculty members in any area of the university. They often are asked by the deans of other colleges within EMU to assist specific faculty members. In an arrangement that Schaub says gives the World College the character of "a collegium," staff members may have several faculty members working with them on release time to develop new expertise and materials.

Much remains to be done to make EMU more global in its perspectives, Schaub says. He hopes, for example, that the university's MBA program can become more international. At the same time, he and his colleagues recognize how dramatically things have changed since the days of plummeting foreign language enrollments in the early 1970s.

Two indicators tell the story. First, graduates of the new Language and International Trade program find jobs. Although the program has always cautioned students that they should expect to be tracked into domestic positions upon graduating, two-thirds of the graduates responding to recent surveys report that they secured internationally focused positions in business within twelve months of graduation. Secondly, and perhaps relatedly, enrollments in the language department are among the most robust in the university. Indeed, the problem now, ironically, is that this university which has never had a traditional language requirement, now has a language department which must turn large numbers of students away.

'The international shingle is out for everybody;
we've made going abroad the thing to do'

KALAMAZOO COLLEGE

Kalamazoo College can make the extraordinary claim that 85 to 90 percent of its graduates study abroad. This has been the case since the early 1960s when, encouraged by a generous patron, the college changed its calendar to make foreign study an integral part of Kalamazoo undergraduate education.

The original impetus for Kalamazoo's foreign study program was the enthusiasm of the chairman of its board, neurosurgeon Richard U. Light. He had seen his four sons derive many benefits from a family vacation in Europe in the late 1950s. During the next five summers, a Light family foundation, the S. R. Light Trust, provided a total of 180 scholarships to selected Kalamazoo students for nine weeks of study in one of three European centers—in Caen, France; Bonn, Germany; and Madrid, Spain.

Careful evaluation showed that the program exceeded even its sponsors' hopes, dramatically increasing students' language proficiency and understanding of different cultures. These findings—and the promise of expanded funding—prompted the college in 1962 to revise its academic calendar so that *all* interested students could benefit. The current calendar makes certain quarters in the four-year schedule of each student available for foreign study—normally the spring quarter of the sophomore year for those choosing to spend one quarter abroad, and the fall and winter quarters of the junior year for the larger group of students preferring to spend more time abroad.

The college has a variety of program options to serve the diverse needs and abilities of its students. One student might elect to study at a university in the United Kingdom for two terms, a semester, or an entire academic year; another might take two quarters (the equivalent of a Western European semester) in France or Germany. "The international shingle is out for everybody," says Joe Fugate, professor of German language and literature, and the long-time director of the Foreign Study Program. "We've made going abroad the thing to do."

The majority of Kalamazoo students abroad are accommodated in one of numerous program sites maintained by the college. These centers currently are located in Aix-en-Provence, Strasbourg, Clermont-Ferrand, and Caen, France; Munster, Hanover, Erlangen, and Bonn, Germany; Madrid and Caceres, Spain; the African nations of Kenya, Sierra Leone, and Senegal; and Ecuador. In virtually all cases, the host sites are foreign institutions that regularly accept Kalamazoo undergraduates. The centers are overseen by local personnel except for visits by program administrators from the U.S., an arrangement that accustoms students to dealing with non-Americans and lowers the college's costs considerably. Where possible, students live with local families. Other study abroad options are available through the Great Lakes Colleges Association and other selected colleges and universities.

The S. R. Light Trust's endowment of a restricted fund to support foreign study has been essential to Kalamazoo's success in helping its students get abroad. Income from this fund enables students to pay only regular on-campus tuition and fee charges during their time abroad (overseas travel costs, usually from New York, are included in these standard charges). In addition, a second quarter abroad costs only one half of the usual college tuition and fees.

The foreign study program is not the only element of the undergraduate experience that gives Kalamazoo its international character. All students must complete a language requirement for intermediate proficiency. Unusually for a college of only twelve hundred undergraduates, Kalamazoo provides language instruction in Chinese, Dutch, classical Greek, Italian, Latin, and Russian, in addition to the three languages—French, German, and Spanish—in which majors are offered. A major and concentration are also offered in international and area studies. Four language houses (French, German, Japanese, and Spanish) are staffed by native-speaking assistants. Students wishing to pursue interests developed while abroad may do so through an internationally oriented career development internship or an individual senior-year project which is required of all students. A grant from the Chamberlain Foundation often provides partial support to students wishing to do these projects overseas.

Fugate and his colleagues are realistic about the challenges ahead: rising costs and recent deficits, faculty members whose own international competence and readiness to work across disciplines need to be developed, and entering students who have had little or no language training in high school. Yet Fugate sees a strong case for continuing the international emphasis. It has made an important difference, he says, for Kalamazoo's students—and the college itself. "When a speaker comes to campus to talk about a remote corner of the world, he or she will draw fifty or sixty people—and often aggressive questioning from students who have been there on our programs," Fugate notes. "We can show a film in a foreign language and get an audience. Maybe most importantly, when we look at

Ramapo College of New Jersey committed itself
to the infusion of an international dimension
throughout its entire program with a process
that is a model of systematic change

---

class reunion books, we see that our graduates often go on to top graduate schools and use their international backgrounds professionally. We see that lives have been changed."

RAMAPO COLLEGE OF NEW JERSEY

The deliberate, formal vocabulary of college and university planning—the terminology of "mission," "goals," "objectives," and "assessments"—can seem remote from the frequent uncertainty, opportunism, and downright messiness of actual institutional reform. Yet the more extensive and complex the reform, the more valuable a well-conceived and well-executed plan is. When Ramapo College of New Jersey committed itself in 1985 to the infusion of an international dimension throughout its entire program, it implemented that commitment with a process that is a model of systematic change.

The rationale for the new direction was largely strategic. Established in 1969 as a four-year, state-supported college with programs in the liberal arts and professional areas, Ramapo had by the mid-1980s seen years of declining enrollments and a loss of public confidence. Ramapo's president, Robert Scott, shared the belief of the college's trustees that the institution lacked a clear identity and sense of purpose—but also that it had distinct strengths and opportunities, including faculty expertise and the campus's proximity to many international firms. These pointed to a new emphasis on global education.

The faculty and administrative planning group brought together by Scott to chart this new course first developed a set of principles to guide its decision making. These held that Ramapo's initiative would emphasize both international and multicultural themes and that these themes should pervade the institution. The new emphasis would inform remedial and developmental courses, general education and area studies, and both liberal arts and professional programs. It would also help to shape the extracurriculum—indeed, all areas of campus life. To be developed where appropriate through partnerships with other organizations, the new global emphasis would even be an important element in the faculty's research and training activities, as well as its undergraduate teaching.

The college translated these principles or goals into six broad objectives, carefully designed to implement the college's mission in the college's markets in ways that would attract the professional interests of the faculty. The first objective was professional development for faculty and staff, with funds for travel, books and materials, consultants, visiting scholars and faculty and staff exchanges as high priorities. The second was curriculum development, to be made possible by release time for revising current courses and developing new ones and for pursuing scholarship and creative endeavors. Skill development was a third broad objective; it encompassed capabilities in languages and computing, as well as international telecommunications, video- and audio-teleconferencing, and television programming. The fourth objective, experiential learning, included such programs as theme dorms, study abroad, student and faculty exchanges, and international cooperative education. Developing programmatic partnerships with other entities and recruiting and retaining students—particularly international and minority students—were the fifth and sixth objectives.

Ramapo focused as much on implementation as on careful goal setting and clear objectives. The first challenge was finding the resources to work with. These came, most notably, in the form of a special three-year, $3.4 million grant from the Governor's Challenge for Excellence Grant Program. According to Scott, however, "The original proposal was structured around a strategic vision that we would have followed with or without the extra state assistance. It also included a four-year financial plan showing how the initiative would be continued after the three-year grant period." Once the grant was awarded, Scott says, faculty and staff members were given assignments of responsibility, a schedule of deadlines, and the assurance that their work would be assessed and rewarded on an annual and sometimes quarterly basis.

Ramapo's progress over the past seven years in fulfilling its original six objectives has been significant. Faculty development, for example, has been particularly successful. Nearly three quarters of the college's full-time faculty members have participated in a series of professional development seminars, including seminars on specific world regions such as Latin America, East Asia, and Africa. Release time has been made available for travel and scholarship. A research institute, the Center for International Education, has been established, and new faculty members have been hired in foreign language and area studies. In addition, about 5 percent of full-time faculty members each year are visiting scholars from other countries—including Fulbright Scholars; an annual scholar supported by the Italian government; Princeton-in-Asia Fellows; members of the editorial staff of Progress Publishers in Moscow; and participants in Ramapo's faculty and foreign scholar exchange programs in Argentina, Volgograd, Puerto

Rico, France, Japan, Italy, China, Taiwan, England, Jamaica, Mexico, and Canada. The college also has been approved to participate in the U.S. State Department's Diplomat-in-Residence program.

To meet the objective of curriculum development, faculty participants in the professional development seminars have created or substantially revised more than seventy courses. These courses are found in every area of the academic program, including developmental reading, general education, honors seminars, and numerous minors and majors. They include new offerings in Italian, Japanese, and Chinese to accompany courses in languages traditionally taught, including Russian.

The decision to offer Italian and Japanese was made largely in recognition of two circumstances. First, in a reflection of the demographics of New Jersey as a whole, more than a third of Ramapo's students are of Italian descent. Second, thousands of New Jersey residents work as managers for the scores of large Japanese-owned corporations located within a fifteen mile radius of the college. Courses in the new languages, supported by library and media acquisitions and the construction of a new language lab, now contribute significantly to Ramapo's language enrollments; overall, these enrollments have nearly quadrupled in recent years.

The development of communications technologies—a distinctive element in Ramapo's plan—also has proceeded apace. Ramapo's new International Telecommunications Center boasts worldwide satellite capabilities for television reception, audio and video conferencing as well as computing, and broadcast-quality television production facilities. These facilities, which serve faculty members and students in all areas of study, have educational potential that is still being discovered. Audio conferencing, for instance, has proven to be a very effective way of assessing the progress of students engaged in study or internships in other countries. The college now can provide telecourses to area community colleges and sixteen school districts and, as a national site for the Satellite Educational Resources Consortium, provide Japanese language tutoring to high schools students.

Some of the most exciting uses of telecommunication, however, are in the classrooms on Ramapo's own campus, including those in which foreign languages are taught. For example, during the Persian Gulf War, hundreds of Ramapo students in regular classes in many different disciplines participated in a live audio conference in which panelists in Italy and Germany discussed European responses to that conflict. Another live audio conference, at a Ramapo-hosted statewide meeting of international educators, featured presentations from several persons at different sites in Brazil, including a village leader and an environmental officer who spoke from the Amazon rainforest.

A highlight of Ramapo's progress toward its goal of expanding experiential learning opportunities for its students has been the development of an international cooperative education program. Through co-op placements in a dozen countries—including Russia, Japan, Germany, and Norway—more than sixty students have earned academic credit for projects directed by a Ramapo faculty member and a host country supervisor. Study abroad, exchange, and routine teleconference opportunities also have been greatly expanded in England, France, Italy, Israel, Japan, Russia, Jamaica, Costa Rica, Mexico, Puerto Rico, Spain, Belgium, and Australia.

To extend outreach activities—its fifth goal—Ramapo has assumed a leading role in providing international and multicultural programs to area high schools, corporations, other colleges and universities, and the northern New Jersey community. For example, the college leads a state-sponsored Project on International and Global Education. It works with Italian and Japanese community groups; offers courses and programs on business, language, and culture to American and foreign employees of international and multinational firms; and is a partner in the New Jersey Center for International Business Education. Scott acknowledges that the college has benefitted from these initiatives, greatly expanding its fundraising potential and results.

Ramapo also has increased the diversity of its own student body and faculty. Thanks in part to new partnership programs with high schools in Newark and other urban centers and articulation agreements with community colleges, foreign student enrollments have increased by more than two hundred percent and minority student enrollments are up more than 60 percent. Retention for these students, now at 80 percent, also has risen steadily. To complement the importation of visiting scholars, the college also has emphasized diversity in faculty recruitment; 40 percent of new faculty appointments in the past six years have gone to minority scholars.

In the last several years, New Jersey's colleges and universities lost more than a third of their state support. Ramapo's international initiatives also have had to do with less. The college has coped by eliminating some activities and staff, reducing library and media purchases, limiting international co-op assignments to those already arranged, and relying more on audio than video teleconferences. Clearly, Ramapo's ability to cut back in

One promising strategy for internationalizing
U.S. colleges and universities is integrating
language study with learning in other
disciplines

---

this area without endangering the continuation of basic reform is due in
large part to the pervasiveness of the initiative—the fact that it is lodged
throughout the college, rather than in one or two vulnerable programs.
There may be lessons in Ramapo's recent experience, then, that bear on
the question of how an international emphasis is sustained in the long
term. As Scott says, "We have had to learn what we can do with money
and what we can do without it."

ST. OLAF COLLEGE

High school and college language requirements bring many students to a
point of intermediate proficiency; then they typically move on to other areas of study—history, chemistry, political science, and so forth—where
they never use their language skills again. One promising strategy for internationalizing U.S. colleges and universities is integrating language study—
and the concomitant development of cross-cultural perspectives—with
learning in other disciplines. A growing number of reformers are suggesting
that students be given more opportunities in courses in other disciplines to
use the language tools they have developed. These opportunities would enable students to consolidate and extend their mastery of their second language and help them attain a richer understanding of other fields.

A successful pioneer of this approach is St. Olaf College, a four-year
undergraduate liberal arts college in Northfield, Minnesota, that enrolls approximately 3,000 students. With the help of a two-year grant (since renewed for three more years) from the National Endowment for the Humanities (NEH) and a three-year grant from the Fund for Improvement of
Postsecondary Education (FIPSE), St. Olaf is enabling students to make significant use of second languages in a range of courses in the humanities,
the behavioral and natural sciences, and mathematics. The college employs several models—ranging from courses "enriched" with foreign language readings to full immersion courses.

St. Olaf students with at least advanced intermediate proficiency in a
foreign language may take courses in other disciplines with an Applied Foreign Language Component (AFLC). In designated AFLC courses, participating undergraduates substitute texts in a foreign language for a number of
the assigned English-language course readings. They also participate in a
special weekly discussion session conducted in that second language, led
jointly by a foreign language department faculty member and the course instructor. Students taking the AFLC option may submit their written work

in English or in the foreign language. Successful completion of two AFLC courses is recognized on student transcripts through the Applied Foreign Language Certification, and each completed AFLC course carries an additional one-quarter course credit.

Early evaluation of the AFLC option indicates that it provides a number of benefits for participating students. Many students report an expanded second language vocabulary and stronger reading comprehension. They value the access they have to important texts not normally studied in language classrooms and sometimes unavailable in English. Students also report special insights into course content, beyond the benefits in understanding that one would expect as a result of spending extra time each week studying a subject.

Keith O. Anderson, professor of German and one of the designers of the AFLC program, draws several examples from a recent course in German history. AFLC students who read course materials in the original language came to understand more fully such key ideas as "Kultur und Bildung" and "Bildungsburgertum"; these terms—essential to an understanding of eighteenth- and nineteenth-century Europe—have nuances and implications obscured by the English translations of "education and culture" and "the educated middle class." Reading about the constitutional convention at the time of the unsuccessful revolution of 1848, students also noted that English texts missed important distinctions among different types of "citizens" referred to in the original documents. Through discoveries like these, says Anderson, AFLC students recognize first-hand "the compromises, judgment calls, distortions and sheer blunders involved in translation"—and thus the importance of reading original texts.

Anderson and his colleagues also point out that students who elect the AFLC option are not its only beneficiaries. Entire classes gain from the deepened level of discussion and increased attention to meaning that result from having some students take advantage of the option.

Participating faculty members credit the AFLC program with helping increase interdisciplinary collaboration and curricular coherence. The NEH grant, for example, supported a core group of fourteen cooperating faculty members as they modified a first set of seven humanities courses to accommodate the AFLC option. The group began its work with a week-long seminar exploring the relationship between foreign language study and the study of other disciplines, and the curricular as well as the pedagogical implications of integrating non-English language texts into the courses of oth-

AFLC students recognize first-hand the
compromises, judgment calls, distortions and
sheer blunders involved in translation—and
thus the importance of reading original texts

er disciplines. Working in pairs on individual courses, the core group then
shaped teaching methods; identified materials for library purchase; selected
appropriate foreign-language texts for course use; and prepared study
guides, glossaries, and other course materials. The participants reported
that this work—sharing ideas about the integration of methods, topics,
and texts and discovering additional sources of information—would influence not simply AFLC courses but all of their teaching.

Anderson and two colleagues who have jointly coordinated the project—Wendy Allen, associate professor of French, and Leon Narvaez, professor of Spanish—also point to benefits that extend beyond the circle of
participating faculty members. Among the faculty as a whole, they report,
the AFLC program has helped generate more discussion about foreign-
language competency and use than has occurred on campus for many
years. A number of faculty members are redeveloping and enhancing their
own foreign-language competency; in the fall of 1990, more than a dozen
non-foreign language faculty members were enrolled in language courses.
In addition, command of a second language has become a factor in the
recruitment of new faculty members. For current language department faculty members themselves, a major benefit of the AFLC approach has been
that it has reaffirmed the critical importance of language study—not merely as the acquisition of a set of formal skills but as an important means of
apprehending other disciplines.

When the AFLC option was created, it was made available to students
in three languages: French, German, and Spanish. Renewed grant support
from NEH has enabled the college to add Russian, Norwegian, and Chinese components to humanities courses as well. An extension into disciplinary domains beyond the humanities has been made possible by the
FIPSE grant, which supports AFLC offerings in the social and natural
sciences.

The AFLC program requires considerable administrative attention.
Twice a year—in April and November—program coordinators send a let-
ter explaining the program to all eligible students. Faculty pairs also visit
second-year language classes to describe the courses they will offer and answer student questions. Although recruiting students in this personal fashion takes time and effort, it is a key element in maintaining the program's
enrollments. Faculty involvement also must be cultivated and encouraged.
A sense of shared ownership is encouraged through a steering committee
that includes faculty members from numerous disciplines. Those who coor-

dinate the program also survey all St. Olaf faculty members each year to update information on their background and interests.

Faculty members who agree to take part in the program receive approximately one month's salary for their preparatory work during the summer. For actually teaching a course with the AFLC for the first time, both members of the faculty pair receive full teaching credit and an honorarium. When they repeat the course, they receive either the honorarium or credit toward an eventual course release. There are now more volunteers among the faculty than there are places for them within the program.

The AFLC program faces challenges. For example, recruitment of faculty members and students in the natural sciences remains difficult. As a matter of policy, the AFLC option has been built into existing courses only, so that its costs are marginal and the program can be more easily sustained. Nonetheless, when grant funds expire, the college will need to meet the ongoing expense of the faculty stipends. These hurdles notwithstanding, AFLC seems to have a strong future at St. Olaf, a college that takes the development of global awareness in its students as a central element of its mission. It also may hold promise for other institutions seeking to strengthen the connection between language study and the rest of the undergraduate enterprise.

UNIVERSITY OF CALIFORNIA, LOS ANGELES

At UCLA, the international focus is not confined to one department or program; it affects the curriculum, research, and student life. This is primarily due to the central coordination provided by the office of International Studies and Overseas Programs (ISOP), established largely through the efforts of one senior faculty champion—James Coleman, then director of the African Studies Center. In 1984 ISOP replaced the Council for International Comparative Studies (ICS), a much looser grouping of area studies centers, and it provides a more coordinated and visible international presence on campus.

ISOP currently oversees and coordinates activities among five area studies centers—for Latin America, Africa, Russia and Eastern Europe, East Asia, and the Near East—as well as the Japan Studies Center, Pacific Rim Center, and Center for International Business. ISOP also houses UCLA's Education Abroad Program (EAP) office and several smaller

At UCLA, the international focus is not
confined to one department or program;
it affects the curriculum, research,
and student life

---

exchange programs, reviews and monitors exchange agreements with institutions abroad, hosts visiting international scholars, and disseminates information.

ISOP is overseen by an executive committee of the area studies directors and a few other key persons, as well as an administrative committee—chaired by the vice chancellor and composed of several deans and the provost—which meets annually to set broad policy for ISOP and monitor all international activities at UCLA. This arrangement enables the university to monitor and coordinate all international activities on the campus and makes international concerns a central part of the university's planning process.

ISOP stimulates internationalization at UCLA not only by coordinating programs but also by providing grants to faculty members to pursue international research and by providing information on other opportunities. By involving faculty members in international research, UCLA encourages the development of international dimensions in all of the university's schools and departments. ISOP recently received the administration's support to hire ten new full-time, tenure-track faculty members with international specializations. The new positions will be allocated among the area studies centers based on need.

Through ISOP, faculty members and students meet each other across disciplines and sometimes start collaborative efforts. On one occasion, a doctoral retreat sponsored jointly by the Center for International Business and the Latin American Studies Center brought together students who saw Latin America from widely divergent angles. Participants included an anthropology student who had lived in a rural village and business students who had worked with Latin American governments on macro-level economic issues. Students were surprised to find how much they had to learn from one another, and what began as a largely suspicious and reticent gathering ended with lively and productive sharing.

About two hundred students from UCLA go abroad to study every year through the Education Abroad Program, the University of California's systemwide international study program. EAP sponsors not only the traditional language and liberal arts programs in Europe but several programs in developing countries, as well as programs for science, engineering, and fine arts students. There is a language requirement for students going to non-English-speaking countries. Soon, students also will be required to take area studies courses in preparation for studying abroad.

Scholarships allow participation by students who otherwise could not afford study abroad and facilitate the participation of under-represented minorities. Students are encouraged to start working with a professor on their senior thesis before going abroad so that they can carry on research while overseas.

Moreover, UCLA is itself a multicultural and international institution. With six thousand international students, two thousand international visiting scholars, and thousands more U.S. students who trace their heritage to all parts of the globe, campus life is inescapably influenced by a variety of cultures. Dozens of culturally based student organizations serve people of common heritage, and for the past three years students have organized a week-long World Fest to bring together all of these groups. Concerts featuring everything from rock to Lithuanian a capella music, food bazaars, art exhibits, and other cultural sharing opportunities bring the different groups together and introduce the campus to the range of cultures present at UCLA. According to Ken Heller, assistant director of the Center for Student Programming (which sponsors World Fest), students sometimes come for one specific group but become more broadly interested when they see, taste, or listen to others' offerings.

The International Student Center—built as a joint community-university venture—gives international students a place to meet with each other and a chance for students and those in the community to interact with them. Panel discussions that feature international students talking about current events in their home countries utilize the wealth of experience that these students have and draw faculty members, community residents, and other students.

An orientation program for international students draws a mixture of volunteers: U.S. nationals, immigrant students, and international students who already have gone through the orientation. These volunteers write to the new international students before they arrive, register them when they arrive, and introduce them to student life at UCLA. In many cases, a student volunteer who is interested in a foreign language can be paired up with an international student of that language to carry on a "language swap."

Max Epstein, dean of international students and scholars, says that UCLA students and faculty members "realize the benefit of interacting with people of other cultures and seek this out." A new International House on campus will increase the visibility of international students at UCLA. Moreover, the decision to make the International Student Center director a dean represents a conscious determination to give international activities a more central place in the university.

UCLA clearly has advantages in internationalizing because of its size, prestige, and multicultural student body. The real key to UCLA's success, however, has been the university's determination to build on its resources—taking advantage of the diversity of its student body, finding links between study-abroad opportunities and the curriculum, and coordinating the existing interest in international issues to increase their visibility and impact on campus.

UNIVERSITY OF CALIFORNIA, SAN DIEGO

At the University of California, San Diego (UCSD), undergraduates complete their general-education requirements within one of five residential colleges, each with a broad but distinctive curriculum and thematic emphasis (such as the environment or social justice). The newest of the five colleges—established in 1988 and known simply as Fifth College—offers an ambitiously international curriculum designed to provide students a coherent, integrated core program emphasizing cross-cultural studies in the humanities, social sciences, and fine arts.

The international focus of Fifth College's general-education requirements does not restrict the student's choice of a major; Fifth College's undergraduates major in all of the twenty-two departments on campus. Nor does this focus mean that students receive instruction from only a small set of faculty members. In addition to holding a departmental appointment, each UCSD faculty member is assigned to or elects affiliation with one of the undergraduate colleges; thanks to this university policy, Fifth College draws on the expertise of ninety-nine faculty members from every academic discipline. In a sense, Fifth College is an academic crossroads for both students and faculty members—established on the assumption that international understanding and competence is multidisciplinary in nature and can be deployed to one's benefit and the benefit of society in virtually any discipline or career.

Like students elsewhere, Fifth College students complete requirements of two courses each in the natural sciences and in mathematics or computer science, and meet an upper-division writing requirement. The international emphasis appears in a stipulation that one of two required fine arts courses must be an exploration of non-Western art, music, or theatre—as well as in a language requirement of a full year, regardless of previous study. Each Fifth College student also must take three courses constituting a "regional specialization" in one of the following geographical areas: Africa; Asia; Europe (classical and medieval, modern, or Russian studies); the Middle East; or Pan-America.

The heart of the Fifth College curriculum, however, is a two-year sequence of six required courses taken in the freshman and sophomore years entitled "The Making of the Modern World." According to James Lyon, founding provost of Fifth College, this distinctive core program involves students in "longitudinal, cross-cultural study of both Western and non-Western civilizations." It employs numerous perspectives from the humanities and social sciences, with history as the integrating discipline. In learning how different traditions developed and led to the modern world, students take courses entitled, "Prehistory and the Birth of Civilization"; "The Great Classical Traditions"; "The Medieval Heritage"; "European Expansion and the Clash of Cultures"; "Revolution, Industry and Empire"; and "Our Century and After." Using an approach that cuts through much contentious national debate about the relative claims of Western and non-Western legacies, the courses all follow both Western and non-Western timelines and emphasize multiple traditions and cultures.

The faculty team that designed the sequence strongly favored using individual instructors rather than team-teaching. Nine of the eleven had participated in team teaching elsewhere; they felt that approach too often left students to integrate what their instructors had not. Instead, individual faculty members are assigned to large lecture sections. With the help of a grant from the Ford Foundation and matching funds from the university, Lyon was able to provide release time for all faculty members who taught during the first three years of the sequence so they could develop command over materials and ideas they were encountering, in many cases, for the first time. Now the release time is totally funded by the university. Lyon also has a cadre of twenty-three experienced faculty members from departments including history, literature, sociology, anthropology, and political science—although he says he would like to augment their number.

Departments find it in their interest to supply faculty members to teach in the sequence because budgets are enrollment-driven in the University of California system; credit for the 150 to 175 students enrolled in each faculty member's lecture section of "The Making of the Modern World" accrues to his or her home department. Departments also regard

Global interdependence requires
a multi-disciplinary approach
which necessarily involves the intersection
of the liberal arts and business

---

the sequence as a source of employment for their graduate students: Each quarter it employs eighteen to twenty teaching assistants to lead the smaller discussion and writing sections that accompany each week's faculty lectures.

Although its large lecture sections are individually taught, the sequence requires extensive faculty collaboration. In any given quarter the three faculty members teaching the same course in the sequence use a common set of readings. Sometimes they teach from a common syllabus; in every case however, they follow the identical course concept, altering only the chronological approach. Prior to each quarter, the three meet together as a team, and those with knowledge of particular texts or issues to be covered coach their colleagues. During the quarter, the three also meet regularly to coordinate their plans. Typically they also draw on one another as occasional guest lecturers—but always with the understanding that it is their responsibility to help their own students integrate the different presentations.

The sequence raises a number of pedagogical issues for those who teach it: What is essential content? What can be left out? How extensive can a reading list be? How should one handle differences among instructors, particularly over ideological approaches? A constant concern is coordination among the different courses in the sequence—and sometimes within them. The second course, for example, examines the Greek culture of the fifth century B.C. side by side with the Han dynasty of China from the third century B.C. to the third century A.D. It also overlaps by several centuries the starting point of the third course, which begins with Imperial Rome and covers the Christian Middle Ages, the T'ang dynasty in China, and the rise and spread of Islam. Instructors in both courses struggle with this inevitable overlap and with the amount they must teach; according to Lyon, each wishes that previous or subsequent quarters would cover more.

Students, too, find the sequence demanding, with its extensive readings, its "primates to postmodernism" sweep, and its substantial writing requirements. They take a special pride, however, in the knowledge and perspective it gives them and see it as an important influence on their subsequent work.

Lyon sees the influence of the Fifth College curriculum reflected in the high percentage of its students and graduates who go abroad. It is to prepare them for that kind of experience that the college insists on language study, he says—pointing out that UCSD also provides students a variety of mechanisms for foreign study. These include the University of California Education Abroad Program (EAP), with affiliates within ninety universities around the globe. In each of the past three years, between 35 and 40 percent of the Fifth College junior class has spent part or all of the junior year abroad, traveling each year to more than thirty countries.

Fifth College is able to provide a strong learning environment because of its integrity as a residential setting and the cohesive cocurricular activity this setting makes possible. As freshmen and sophomores, Fifth College students live together in their own residence halls and apartments. Activities there and in the nearby UCSD International House emphasize international understanding and exchange—including, for example, national theme days or evenings; multicultural festivals of film, music, dance, and food; and world affairs speakers and discussions.

Asked to what extent he thinks other institutions could replicate UCSD's accomplishments, Lyon points out how rare an opportunity he and his Fifth College colleagues had in their ability "to start from scratch, with funding." The mid-1980s were a time of rapid faculty expansion as well, when growing departments allowed him to be involved in recruitment and gave him commitments of cooperation. At other places, he says, "you might have to move the cemetery. Even so, the ideas, the concepts behind the courses—parts of what we did will travel."

UNIVERSITY OF MICHIGAN

What we mean by global interdependence...transcends merely the economic interdependence of nations, which is already a commonplace. It involves also the complex interdependence of economic, political, historical, geographical and cultural forces at the firm, national, and international levels. In short, the understanding and management of global interdependence is inherently a multi-disciplinary problem. It requires a multi-disciplinary approach which necessarily involves the intersection of the liberal arts and business....

So writes economist Linda Lim in the course guide to "Global Interdependence," an interdisciplinary course she now teaches at the University of Michigan. Originally conceived by her colleague Kenneth De Woskin, a professor of Asian languages and cultures, the course draws extensively on

One aspect of the course that students reported appreciating was its capacity to challenge their accustomed world views

---

lectures by different faculty specialists on their areas of expertise; the course as a whole is a resolutely general introduction to its subject.

Developed as an initiative of the University's Center for International Business Education and Research (CIBER), "Global Interdependence" casts a broad net with respect to students, faculty members, and subject matter. Lim and De Woskin believed that all students, no matter what their discipline, need a basic knowledge of how global society's interactions have become, and how they are conditioned by factors that are traditionally studied only in separation—within the humanities, the sciences, the social sciences, and the different professional areas. Although Michigan students could previously explore important international topics, the opportunity often was reserved for those who were willing to do relatively in-depth study and who had met prerequisites in economics, especially. The university, Lim and De Woskin concluded, needed a course that would cover global interdependence broadly and be open to nonspecialists from any part of campus. The course they designed has no prerequisites, is open to graduate students and upper-level undergraduates, and counts toward the university's undergraduate general-education requirements.

Rather than trying to teach this broad course singlehandedly or together, Lim and De Woskin embraced another strategy for staffing. They identified faculty members who had expertise in areas they wanted the course to cover and who were known to be able lecturers. Ultimately, they invited sixteen professors to join them in teaching the course. It would be, in Lim's phrase, "a circus course," built around a semester-long series of twenty-six lectures shared among the faculty members—with enough provisions built in, Lim and De Woskin hoped, to help students integrate the many different perspectives to which they would be exposed.

The resulting course has extraordinary sweep and intellectual interest. Two introductory lectures that frame the key concerns of the course are followed by five units of four to six lectures each. The first, "The History of International Trade," draws on lecturers from Asian languages and culture, history, political science, and business administration who address topics such as "The China Trade: From the Silk Route to the Opium Wars" and "Slavery, Race and Plantation Societies: Colonialism in the Caribbean." The second unit, "International Economic Relations," brings in other instructors from business administration, sociology, and the Center for Research on Economic Development; it explores U.S.-Japan trade, Europe after 1992, and economic development in Eastern Europe and Africa, among other topics. In "Culture and International Competition," the third unit, another multidisciplinary team (including a psychologist) addresses the tensions between religion and economic systems—exploring, for example, Confucianism and capitalism in East Asia, the effects on women of the international division of labor, and the connections between education and international competitiveness.

A fourth set of issues—including the international spread of AIDS, global environmental change, and communications technology ("the CNN factor," Lim explains) are explored in the next unit, "One World: Technology, Health and Environment." Here, faculty members from natural resources, epidemiology and international health, physics, and communications and political science provide the lectures. The fifth and final section of the course is a concluding set of two lectures—the first entitled "The Multinational Corporation" and the second "Managing Global Interdependence: Follow-up Courses and Career Options."

The first time the course was taught, Lim—a Singapore-born economist who teaches international business as a Southeast Asia specialist—found herself overextended in her role as course coordinator. She recruited and scheduled faculty members, attended all lectures (and gave several), graded all papers and exams, and met a heavy demand by students for consultations outside of class. The students, for their part, were intensely interested in the course's content but struggled to link its parts and see the complex connections among them. What they learned, Lim's careful evaluation showed, was largely factual; they did not learn as well that "way of looking at the world, of thinking" that she and her colleagues hoped to impart.

To rectify these problems, Lim modified the course in key ways. She reduced the number of lectures and introduced a discussion session at the end of each unit. Having this additional time to think collectively through what they have heard in lecture has helped students focus more on broad issues and on synthesis and integration. It also has reduced their need for individual conferences with Lim to discuss paper topics. Ideally, she says, a discussion session would follow every lecture. The students themselves would resist that change, however; far from wanting the number of lectures to be reduced, most respondents to her survey wanted to see more topics introduced and the course expanded to two semesters.

One aspect of the course that students reported appreciating was its capacity to challenge their accustomed world views. Most students in class were liberal arts majors, and many had attitudes that might be considered "anti-business." Lim says the course has led students to "consider a world in which both former socialist and developing countries are embracing capitalism, free markets, foreign investment and international trade more enthusiastically than ever before. Not only have students had to think more analytically about economic and other social issues," Lim continues, "but they have even been encouraged to rethink their own career directions in light of problems they studied." Students who took the course, she says, may be more open to the idea not only that business is a major factor in world affairs today but that it is necessary force for progressive change in everything from cleaning up the environment to improving the economic position of women in developing countries.

The CIBER grant that has supported Lim's involvement and paid honoraria for the participating faculty members has been renewed for three more years; meanwhile, Lim and De Woskin continue working to establish the course on more permanent footing. They hope that funding will be available to support somewhat smaller honoraria that would be needed for faculty members to update their lectures for new audiences, and that the College of Literature, Science and the Arts—which offers the course and contributes a part-time grader—will continue to expand its cost-sharing.

The course is replicable, Lim and De Woskin contend, either at individual colleges or through consortia of neighboring institutions. They are preparing a book of course readings for use on other campuses that might be interested in a similar course but do not have so wide an array of specialists to call upon. With funding from the KPMG Peat Marwick Foundation, moreover, she and other faculty members associated with the course have begun working directly with colleagues from Tuskegee University. Faculty members at this historically black institution in Alabama are interested in adapting "Global Interdependence" to the particular needs and resources of their own campus. The idea, Lim says, "is flexible. Every school has faculty members with international expertise. It's largely a matter of cobbling them together in a way that makes sense and remembering the students' guidance and integration."

UNIVERSITY OF PENNSYLVANIA

The University of Pennsylvania's Joseph H. Lauder Institute offers a two-year program leading to an MBA from the Wharton School and an M.A. in international studies from the university's School of Arts and Sciences.

To page through the biographical summaries in the institute's directory of current students is to realize, however, that beginners need not apply. The fifty or so students selected for Lauder each year already are unusually international in outlook and background.

One current student, for example, is a German-born Princeton graduate (with a B.A. in comparative politics). She spent her junior year in Paris, directed marketing for a trade and consulting firm that focused on business development in the Soviet Union, and she speaks fluent French, Hebrew, and Italian as well as some German, Russian, and Spanish. Another Lauder student is a Nigerian man who graduated from Oxford with a B.A. in engineering science and economics and from Columbia with an M.S. in electrical engineering; after working as an insurance industry analyst in New York, he has devoted himself to developing expertise in East Asia and the Japanese language through further study at Middlebury College and the International University of Japan.

These two are typical of their classmates in the diversity of their backgrounds as well as their demonstrated interest and competence in the international realm. Other characteristics of Lauder students include an average age of 26.5 years, an average of 3.5 years of work experience, and high average undergraduate grade point averages (3.4) and GMAT scores (640). Nearly a third of all Lauder students are non-U.S. citizens, and all, upon entry, have demonstrated at least "advanced" (ACTFL level 2) proficiency in a second language.

John Farley, the Ira Lipman Professor at Wharton and Lauder's director, explains that the threshold of language proficiency is set high because cultural seminars are conducted in the students' language of study. Lauder therefore seeks to help MBA students who already have language skills to capitalize on them and continue to develop them further. "Superior professional" command (ACTFL level 3) is expected of all students by the time they graduate—a significant accomplishment given the other demands of the program.

Not merely a joint degree program but one that integrates the study of business and the arts and sciences, the Lauder curriculum begins with a summer session and extends over a total of twenty-four months. Each newly admitted class first completes two concurrent month-long courses, two MBA core mini-courses in management and marketing, and a required M.A. course in comparative economics and politics. The class then divides into groups for study abroad during the rest of the summer. Groups depart for Beijing, Moscow, Munich, Paris, Puebla (Mexico), Sao Paulo, and Tokyo. While abroad, students receive eight weeks of language and cultural instruction from local professors and take part in visits to corporations and cultural excursions. Non-U.S. citizens studying English remain in Philadelphia.

In the ensuing academic year, Lauder students take six MBA core courses (in areas such as accounting, business policy, and financial analysis), two economics courses that are jointly credited toward both the M.A. and the MBA, and four more courses that satisfy M.A. requirements only. Two of the M.A. courses continue a sequence of language and cultural perspective courses that runs through the program; these courses integrate language study with the study of contemporary and traditional cultures, including management communication styles, behaviors, and protocols in a range of professional and social settings. Each student's sequence focuses on one of the several regional and language specializations offered: Western Europe (French or German), Latin America (Spanish or Portuguese), East Asia (Chinese or Japanese), the U.S. (English as a second language), or Eastern Europe and the former Soviet Union (Russian). The other two M.A. courses taken during this first year include a history course on the student's region of specialization and an approved arts and science elective, which might be in any of several areas as diverse as economics, law, religion, technology, politics, or the arts.

Also during the academic year, Lauder Institute staff members work to bring representatives of international corporations to campus, where they interview members of the first-year class as prospective summer interns. All Lauder students eventually choose an internship that pays them for twelve weeks of work with a company in the region they are studying.

The second year's curriculum brings more MBA work—most of it now in the student's Wharton major—and a jointly credited course in management, finance, or marketing that is taught from an international perspective. Joint credit also is given in the spring semester for an advanced study project—a research paper that usually explores a business topic within a sociocultural context. The remaining M.A. work is in the language and cultural perspective sequence, arts and sciences electives, and—in the final semester—a capstone seminar.

Lauder graduates are in considerable demand. Seven cohorts have finished the program to date, and their members are now employed in U.S.

corporations with substantial business abroad, such as Citibank, Banker's Trust, American Express, and McKinsey, and in foreign-based firms such as The Sakora Bank and Deutsche Bank. Graduates may wait a year or two for foreign assignments, but in most cases they can begin to employ their international training quickly. For example, of the twenty-six graduates who have studied Japanese at Lauder, says Farley, at least nineteen already are using that language in their work.

The Lauder Institute has enviable resources beyond its affiliations with an Ivy League university and an elite business school. It was established in 1983 with an endowment from Leonard and Ronald Lauder and enjoys both government and private support. Its board of governors includes CEOs from multinational corporations who contribute to the program in a variety of ways (among them by serving as guest speakers in a special non-credit component of the Lauder curriculum, the International Executive Lecture Series). Its staff includes a director (always a Wharton faculty member with a strong commitment to international education); a co-director; a business manager; and four assistant directors in external affairs, development, language and culture, and student affairs and admissions.

The institute occupies two floors equipped with a language laboratory, language seminar rooms, and a library resource room in a handsome new building on the Penn campus, Lauder-Fischer Hall. The centerpiece of this state-of-the-art facility—and the greater part of the institute's floor space—is an auditorium and a lounge equipped with a large screen television on which, at all hours, Lauder students gather to watch foreign-language news programs beamed in via satellite on the SCOLA channel. Each language group has its accustomed time, says Farley. "If it's 2:00 p.m., you'll see the Russian speakers."

These assets notwithstanding, administering Lauder has its challenges. With its pervasive interdisciplinarity, Farley says, the institute frequently runs afoul of systems that were created for more simply structured programs. Even the extraordinary commitment and self-directedness of the Lauder students can, on a bad day, seem too much of a good thing. "It isn't always easy," says Farley, "to satisfy a hundred highly motivated graduate students, each wishing to follow his or her own plan."

Although Lauder provides a model for the integration of advanced foreign language instruction and area studies with graduate study in business, the institute's structure probably is less widely replicable than other programs featured in these pages. Yet its work is clearly of some interest na-

Several German professors at URI have
accepted the challenge to extend the language
learning experience to new subject areas and to
the needs of a broader group of students

---

tionally. The U.S. Department of Education has designated the institute as the core of the first National Resource Center in International Studies for Management. As such, the institute already is helping to train faculty members and assist in the development of curriculum materials for other colleges and universities.

UNIVERSITY OF RHODE ISLAND

Like their colleagues on other campuses, German professors at the University of Rhode Island are accustomed to teaching language courses with a literature focus; a typical course might involve guiding a group of liberal arts students through a close study of Goethe or Kafka. Though literature still is a large part of their program, several German professors at URI have accepted the challenge to extend the language learning experience to new subject areas and to the needs of a broader group of students.

For the last five years, URI faculty members have taught a sequence of German classes composed entirely of—and designed entirely for—undergraduate engineers. These courses stress oral skills and everyday, rather than literary, German. They also integrate basic vocabulary from fields such as physics, computer science, chemistry, and especially mathematics.

"It is unusual, and sometimes taxing," says one experienced instructor, "for those of us who have long since dismissed algebra from daily thought to see the blackboard of German 101 filled with geometric shapes or mathematical formulas." Still, it is refreshing to replace "ein kleines Madchen" or "ein grunes Buch" with "ein positives Vorzeichen" or "rechtwinkliges Dreieck." Eventually, the mathematics outstrips the ability of the German faculty to teach it; by the third or fourth semester of the six-course sequence, mathematicians or German-speaking engineering professors or graduate students are called upon to help with the calculations.

This unusual sequence of language courses is offered through URI's International Engineering Program (IEP). IEP enables students to combine the study of German with engineering and to graduate after five years with both a B.S. in an engineering discipline and a B.A. in German. The key elements of the program are the tailored German-language courses over the first three years of study; a six-month paid internship in an engineering firm or research institute in a German-speaking country during the fourth year; and, in the fifth year, both traditional upper-level German language and literature courses and a special interdisciplinary engineering course taught in German by bilingual engineering faculty members.

The ideas behind IEP arose out of casual conversation between Hermann Viets, formerly URI's dean of engineering, and John M. Grandin, professor of German and chair of the department of modern and classical languages and literatures, who now directs the initiative. They were concerned that most of the university's graduates, like most Americans, were culture-bound and monolingual. They formed a joint foreign language and engineering committee to explore the feasibility of a new program in which the engineering and arts and sciences schools could work together on the problem. This committee ultimately shaped a proposal for FIPSE, and when the proposal was funded in August 1987, the program was launched immediately.

Program planners had several reasons for selecting German as the language to be taught in the new joint degree program. The university's German department was committed to teaching German for the professions, and the college of engineering could provide six faculty members who were fluent in German (and enthusiastic about the new program). Moreover, URI already was the home of the German Summer School of the Atlantic, a residential, total-immersion program subsidized by the Federal Republic of Germany.

German also seemed a particularly wise choice as a second language for engineering students in light of Germany's importance as a trading partner of the U.S. and its position as a leader in high technology. A final factor was the existence of more than two thousand subsidiaries of German firms in the U.S.—many of them in or near Rhode Island. The program planners expected that these firms might provide numerous possibilities for internships.

Since most engineering majors graduate in four years and are adequately challenged by their own curriculum, program planners wondered how the new offering—a longer, more expensive program requiring mastery of a difficult language—would be received. To their astonishment, a quick sequence of late-summer mailings yielded forty-seven enrollments—considerably more than the fifteen they had planned for. By the second year, the special demands of the program and other circumstances had lowered the number in this cohort to twenty-five, and attrition has continued at more moderate rates in years three, four, and five. The pattern now seems to be that about 20 percent of any year's freshman engineers will begin the program, and about one third of that group will complete it. To date, twenty students have graduated from the program; all have either gone to work for international companies or have chosen to extend their studies in graduate programs.

One factor that encourages students to persevere is that, from the outset, each IEP class experiences the program as a group. Remaining together helps participating students maintain their awareness of common academic and professional goals and overcome academic hurdles confronting them. In their language classes, the topics, guest speakers, and readings and other materials can be oriented to their special interests and needs—not the least of which is readiness, after three short years, for a technical internship in which German will be the only language spoken.

Faculty members and students regard that internship as the focal point of the program. It is a key motivation for students in the first three years, as well as a powerful educational experience that brings each student's interests and preparations together. It also has been one of the most challenging elements of the program to arrange and administer. Working through new and preexisting contacts both here and abroad, the program directors gradually have developed a growing international network of businesses willing to offer placements. Recent internships have taken students to Munich, for example, to work at Siemens and to Friedrichshafen to work at the Zahnradfabrik, a major automobile gear and transmission manufacturer. Four other firms—American companies with German partners and German companies with subsidiaries in Rhode Island—recently have extended the program's original design; they employ promising students as summer interns in Rhode Island after the freshmen and sophomore years, with the intention of preparing them still better for their internships abroad. To date, IEP has sent twenty-five students to engineering internships in Germany.

The program's final element—the fifth year engineering-in-German course—is offered every other year. Students receive credit for this both as a German course and as a professional engineering elective. Although the course has been offered quite successfully, it presents its own challenges to the German-speaking engineering professors who teach it. Since they typically come from different disciplines within engineering, they sometimes must update their knowledge in each other's fields and struggle to find common problem-solving exercises. Finding German-language materials appropriate for class discussion—for example, articles on current technological issues in the German press—also can be elusive.

Like their peers on other campuses who direct programs launched with outside funding, Grandin and his colleagues work to find ways to maintain what has been created. Grandin has never had to buy the time of faculty members in the German department; they have participated enthusiastically, and the university has credited their efforts in the course. Nonetheless, release time will have to be granted to the faculty member who manages the overall program, from student recruitment to career placement, and this and other expenses will require a continuing commitment of university resources, external funding, or both. The program's close cooperation with private enterprise gives it realistic hope for growing support from that quarter.

While Grandin and his colleagues in both German and engineering have begun studying the possible expansion of IEP into other language areas—including French, Chinese, and Japanese—he has launched a similar initiative to be carried out in cooperation with URI's college of business administration. With a seed grant provided by KPMG Peat Marwick in the recent AAC/AACSB-administered competition, URI is helping its German faculty learn business skills and its business faculty learn German in preparation for six-semester, team-taught sequences of German courses focusing on issues pertinent to careers in international business.

Grandin and Professor Chai Kim of the business school have expanded upon these ideas and secured funding for the next two years through the U.S. Department of Education's Undergraduate International Studies and Foreign Language Program. The result has been a strong move toward internationalization of the undergraduate business curriculum. Faculty members are creating international components to be integrated into each of the core courses in the business curriculum and, simultaneously, into selected French and German courses. Over the past two years, nine business faculty members have enrolled in intensive language courses in France and Germany.

The college of business administration is increasingly committed to international and foreign language education. The business faculty voted recently to introduce a language requirement for all students in their programs. With the strong support of Dean Sydney Stern, faculty members also are strongly encouraging students planning careers in business to consider a five-year B.A./MBA program: four years of undergraduate work with a language major and business minor, a summer internship with a firm abroad, and an intensive one-year MBA. Finally, discussions are underway

The German faculty at URI believe
that language learning must be integrated
into the disciplines of all students
and taught across the curriculum

with European institutions to explore the possibility of graduate-level work
leading to degrees from both URI and those universities.

The German faculty at URI, reports Grandin, no longer think of their
field as a monodimensional one that takes literary study as its single goal.
They believe that language learning must be integrated into the disciplines
of all students and taught across the curriculum. They regard the International
Engineering Program and the Business-Language Program as proof
that this can be done. The outcome, Grandin says, is "not only a richer
educational experience for the student but an enrichment for the faculty
involved who gain a much clearer appreciation for each other's disciplines.
URI has found international education to be the centerpiece around which
faculty members from traditionally disparate areas can gather with very productive
results."

UNIVERSITY OF SOUTH CAROLINA

When the University of South Carolina decided to internationalize its business
school in 1974, it started by creating an entirely new program to
combine business education, area studies, and foreign language in a new
graduate degree: the Masters of International Business Studies (MIBS).
According to MIBS founder William Folks, the faculty and administration
were convinced that "the globalization of business is a major structural
change in the way companies do business, and, therefore, it requires a
strategic change in the business school curriculum."

The leaders of this effort wanted to create more than just an internationalized
MBA; they wanted an entirely new structure that would teach
students how to function in an international environment. The foreign language
faculty—facing the backlash against foreign language study that was
prevalent in the 1970s—responded enthusiastically to the idea, and the
area studies faculty joined in as well. Within a few years, the MIBS program's
tenured international business faculty had increased from three to
ten members and the number of languages it offered had grown from two
(Spanish and German) to six (including French, Portuguese, Arabic, and
Japanese). Today, students can choose Korean, Italian, and Russian as
well, and next year Mandarin Chinese will be added.

MIBS students begin the program with an intensive summer course in
their chosen language. In the fall and spring semesters, they take mostly
business classes. Those who do not have an undergraduate business degree
take the regular MBA core courses plus a set of internationalized MBA

courses; those with previous business education take only the internationalized MBA courses and a set of international business electives. In May and June, MIBS students take a series of area studies courses on the political and social structure of their chosen region of the world. According to Folks, the area studies, language, and business courses are essential and coordinated elements in a program that prepares students to function effectively in a different culture.

After the area studies courses, students leave South Carolina to go abroad. Students who elect to study German, Spanish, French, or Portuguese spend the summer in intensive language programs in Germany, Costa Rica, France, or Brazil, and then in a five-and-a-half to six-month business internship in a country where the language is spoken. After the winter break, students return to campus to finish a final semester of business and area studies classes.

Students studying one of the less commonly taught languages take a three-year program. Students of Arabic, Japanese, and Korean spend a year studying at a university in Cairo, Tokyo, or Seoul before completing their internship in those countries. Students whose language of choice is Chinese study in Taiwan, then at the University of International Business in Beijing, before doing an internship in the People's Republic of China.

About 20 percent of MIBS students are foreign nationals; they take an American studies program instead of a language program—fluent English is a requirement for admission—and do their internship in a U.S.-based corporation.

The internationalization of South Carolina's business programs doesn't stop with MIBS. Folks and others had planned MIBS, in part, to help stimulate a wide range of international activities at South Carolina. Today, for example, more than a quarter of South Carolina's MBA students are foreign nationals. According to Folks, "If you walk into our MBA class, it's like walking into a joint meeting of the EC and the North American Free Trade Association." As a result, even students who never leave the state get an international flavor to their education. South Carolina also sponsors undergraduate study-abroad programs in business in Helsinki and Vienna.

International research has been another priority at South Carolina. The International Business Center provides grants for interdisciplinary research; there are several joint international research efforts between

The globalization of business is a major
structural change in the way companies do
business, and, therefore, it requires a strategic
change in the business school curriculum

---

business and liberal arts faculty members. For eight years, South Carolina
published the *Journal of International Business Studies*, as well as its own
working paper series.

To share some of its success with other institutions, South Carolina
operates faculty development programs for faculty members and administrators at other campuses. "Faculty Development in International Business,"
a series of two-week classes, attracts more than eighty faculty members
each summer. Most take two of the eight courses offered, which take participants through a sample internationalized business course and offer
pointers on how to teach the material and where to find resources. The
Eastern European Program gives faculty members with an interest in Eastern and Central Europe a chance to learn about integrating that area of
the world into their business curriculum during a two-week course in Vienna, Budapest, and Prague. South Carolina also offers a three-day course,
"Administrative Strategies for Internationalizing the Business School,"
that gives administrators ideas for strategic planning.

Plans for the future include a joint Law and International Business
degree, an undergraduate area studies major with a business emphasis, and
a multicultural MBA, half of which will be taught at Universität WWW in
Vienna and half at South Carolina. The University's primary mission remains serving the state of South Carolina, and Folks sees the international
emphasis as very much in the state's interests. "International education is
natural because much of the product in South Carolina is exported and
much of the investment base is foreign.... We have historically been very
integrated into the international economy."

Since the 1970s, an international vision has been integrated into the
overall strategic plan of the university. The MIBS program is an example
of a reform effort that generated significant support from the academic
departments and the campus at large. Significant resources in the form of
faculty positions and a specialized degree program were obtained over a
number of years. As a result, the program has gained national recognition
and become one of the most distinctive characteristics of the university.

WORCESTER POLYTECHNIC INSTITUTE

The sciences and engineering may be less receptive to international education than all other areas of the academic enterprise. Universities sometimes teach these disciplines as if their practice were independent of societies and cultures, and the prescribed, tightly structured character of their

curricula makes it difficult for undergraduate scientists and engineers to find appropriate time or opportunities for foreign study.

Worcester Polytechnic Institute (WPI), a private technological university in Worcester, Massachusetts, is not unlike other institutions of its type; approximately 75 percent of its 2,850 undergraduates are engineering majors, and the remainder are majoring in the sciences and management. Yet foreign study is thriving at WPI. In a required junior-year project, the institution has found a particularly effective means not only of providing interested students with experience abroad but also of extending and enriching their disciplinary education.

The liberal education of engineers and scientists is a traditional and vital commitment at WPI. WPI's distinctive curriculum, in place since the early 1970s, is designed to develop in students not only technical proficiency but an understanding of human social values as well. Fully a quarter of the curriculum—almost twice the amount at most engineering schools—is devoted to the humanities, social sciences, and interdisciplinary studies.

Among other requirements, each student must complete in the junior year an Interactive Qualifying Project (IQP). Carrying nine hours of credit, the IQP challenges students to define, study, and recommend solutions to real-world problems arising out of the interaction of science and technology with societal values, structures, and needs. Students may complete their IQPs either on or off campus; the projects often are sponsored by professional, educational, or governmental organizations that benefit directly from the students' findings and recommendations.

Within WPI's unique academic calendar, juniors begin preparing part-time for the IQP during one of the year's four seven-week terms. Working under close faculty supervision, the students complete the project working full-time during the term that follows. This arrangement entails minimum interruption or postponement of disciplinary course sequences, even for students doing IQPs off campus.

Because of its timing and duration, the IQP lends itself to international study, but few students would choose to tackle projects abroad were it not for other types of support. The first factor is the enthusiasm of the faculty—for whom the supervision of IQPs is a basic teaching responsibility. According to William Grogan, dean emeritus of undergraduate studies and architect of the current curriculum, some faculty members initially took a "What's in it for me?" attitude toward the IQP requirement. As more facul-

The liberal education of engineers and scientists
at WPI is designed to develop in students not
only technical proficiency but an understanding
of human social values as well

ty members have advised IQP teams working in foreign settings, however, they have discovered its value in broadening their own personal and professional horizons; in fact, there now is a waiting list of prospective IQP advisors.

A second essential support has been the growing international network of project centers and programs—staffed by adjunct or full-time WPI faculty members—in Europe (England, Ireland, and Italy) and Asia (Thailand, Hong Kong, and Taiwan). Two new centers soon will begin operation in this hemisphere—one in Puerto Rico, the other in Ecuador. In addition to these project centers and programs, WPI also has an array of bilateral educational exchange agreements with institutions in Germany, France, Switzerland, and Sweden and membership in the International Student Exchange Program, both of which multiply the number of sites at which WPI students can undertake projects.

A third type of support is financial. The additional cost to the student of an IQP abroad tends to average about $2,600—primarily the result of transportation and a living cost differential. This expense is made more manageable in several ways. WPI recognizes the increased expenses of foreign study in financial aid packages and waives on-campus residence hall fees for the term abroad. If the student must travel to the Far East, moreover, industry sponsors often pick up much of the cost of travel beyond the West Coast of the U.S. Support from such external sponsors helps make possible other IQPs abroad as well: Xerox Corporation, for example, is sponsoring the new project center in Puerto Rico, and the Agency for International Development and UNESCO are helping support programs in Ecuador and Venice, respectively. WPI bears the cost of faculty advisors, who are in residence at the major centers or who make visits to the smaller IQP sites at the beginning and end of the project, but even these expenses often are met partly out of a grant support and other sponsorship.

WPI conceives of foreign study as a form of purposeful service learning. Especially given their fields of professional training, WPI students in many cases can make very practical contributions. The list of recent projects abroad includes studies of the safety regulations governing high-rise apartment construction in Hong Kong, the societal impact of Taipei's new mass transit system, and the public policy implications of a toxic spill in the Rhine River. One team even produced a feasibility study of the Venice project center for the IQP program itself.

International IQPs differ in the extent to which they require foreign language skills. As a matter of WPI policy, all students going to Switzerland and Germany are required to know some German, and those going to Ecuador and Puerto Rico will need to have Spanish. Some WPI students, of course, have studied these languages in high school, and those wishing to may use language courses taught at WPI or nearby campuses to meet their humanities requirement. In the Orient, projects are prepared in English, although care is taken to see that teams include native speakers.

WPI efforts to encourage projects abroad have met with considerable success. This year, about 30 percent of WPI juniors are doing their IQPs at foreign sites. The engineering majors among them constitute fully 10 percent of the engineering majors nationally who are studying in other countries. Some persistent barriers to higher rates of participation remain, however—particularly for those who play intercollegiate sports, serve as residential advisors, or hold part-time jobs. For them, however, Summer Term projects are available in London and Venice. Program administrators think a 50 percent rate is achievable.

According to Grogan, more students are coming to WPI because of the IQP program. Whatever their reason for choosing WPI, those students who go abroad not only make WPI a more globally oriented institution when they return, but they encourage other students to consider international IQPs as well. Another unanticipated but important side benefit of WPI's globalization program has been the opportunity to coordinate it with the on-campus diversity program, mutually reinforcing both efforts.

LESSONS FROM CAMPUS PRACTICE

BY RICHARD J. EDELSTEIN

THERE IS NO ONE BEST APPROACH

The profiles in the previous section suggest that there is no single best model for initiating international and interdisciplinary programming on campus. The institutions and programs described exhibit a variety of approaches to internationalization. In part, of course, this reflects the diversity of institutions represented, their different modes of organization, their different cultures, their varying educational philosophies, and their diverse resources.

Good planning and astute implementation strategies can help to ensure program success. The grand design of the Fifth College at the University of California, San Diego and the comprehensive approach developed by Ramapo State College represent highly organized planning. More ad hoc, incremental, or idiosyncratic efforts are found in UCLA's ISOP center or the College of Staten Island's Commerce and Culture program. These characterizations are, of course, oversimplified: The evolution of each program involved some planning and thoughtful analysis of strategic options, as well as arbitrary decisions, ad hoc revisions, and plain old good luck. Most initiatives are guaranteed to be rather messy—although they are unlikely to be successful without some strategic planning and thoughtful leadership.

To suggest that there are multiple models or strategies for successful implementation of international programs is not to imply, however, that the efforts profiled have little in common. Each effort appears to address a common set of issues or problems—in its own way. Furthermore, the obstacles facing planners working on internationalization are similar to those faced by any initiative to reform university curricula, pedagogical approaches, or modes of organization. The substantial body of literature on organizational change is relevant whether the problem is developing a course on global interdependence in a business school or integrating an international internship option into a college of letters and sciences.

KNOW YOUR INSTITUTION

Burton Clark describes the university as a "complex web of disciplinary interests."[1] Although the degree to which colleges and universities are

In almost all the cases profiled, the active support of senior administrators—presidents, provosts, deans—has been critical

---

driven by departmental and disciplinary interests varies, understanding the significance of departments, colleges, and disciplinary groupings is critical to designing and implementing a successful interdisciplinary program at any institution.

An organizational assessment of some sort is required. International curricula and programming by definition are interdisciplinary. Trying to develop collaborative efforts between two or more departments or schools that have a history of troubled relations obviously would not be a productive strategy. Choosing individual faculty members, administrators, and departments with which to work can be a critical strategic factor. Taking the time to assess how the college and university is organized—and the consequent implications for selecting participants, collaborators, and implementation strategies—is essential. In most of the cases profiled above, the individuals who created the programs were sophisticated observers of the organizational culture and political, cultural, and organizational idiosyncrasies of their institutions.

The difficulties of collaborating across departmental boundaries also are rooted in epistemological, methodological, and philosophical differences that challenge the intellectual basis for collaborative work. Efforts to join liberal arts departments and professional schools and programs can be especially demanding.

Finally, there are more mundane and pragmatic reasons for tensions between academic groupings on campus. All departments compete for resources; in most institutions, this implies the capacity to generate student demand for courses and teachers. Decisions regarding which department or faculty member will receive credit for teaching an interdisciplinary course, for example, can be an incentive or a disincentive for agreeing to collaborate across department lines.

ATTEND TO THE CHALLENGE OF PEDAGOGY

The pedagogy of interdisciplinary and international curricula may be the most challenging constraint on the creation of these programs. Integrating material and concepts from different disciplines, integrating the internship or study abroad experience into the larger curriculum, or introducing foreign language elements into advanced courses in business or engineering present complex intellectual and pedagogical demands. Indeed, the pedagogy of interdisciplinary and international curricula is still being invented. Although the challenges are great, the programs profiled in the previous section provide numerous hints and ideas about what types of strategies and models are likely to be most successful.

LEADERSHIP MAKES A DIFFERENCE

The success of each of the programs profiled is related to the efforts of an individual faculty member or administrator who championed the program and was politically astute enough to guide the project around myriad obstacles to successful implementation. Each program had a leader or a group of advocates who had a vision and invested significant time and energy in organizing campus support, raising funds, and shepherding the program through the various stages of development and implementation.

Program "champions" in the profiles include a wide range of individuals. At Ramapo College, for example, the president of the institution was active in defining the need and establishing the objectives of the multiple programs that were initiated. At the University of California, San Diego's Fifth College, the provost was a focal point for action. A faculty member and a dean at the business school were influential in the development of the MIBS program at the University of South Carolina. At the University of Michigan, a key faculty member was a driving force behind the creation of a new course. Kalamazoo College and the Lauder Institute at the University of Pennsylvania represent instances in which leadership, at least in part, came from outside the faculty in the form of a trustee or benefactor.

In fact, program champions can come from almost anywhere in the institution: administration, faculty, students, alumni, trustees. What is critical is that the individuals involved have the status, authority, and respect of colleagues necessary to develop support for the program—and that they know how to build commitments and coalitions across the campus. Gaining the support of a diverse group of key individuals at different levels and in different disciplines is one of the most salient ingredients of successful programs.

In almost all the cases profiled, the active support of senior administrators—presidents, provosts, deans—has been critical. Although individual faculty members or program administrators may have created the program, the support of the president or senior academic officer usually has been vital at key points in its development. When institutional resources are at stake and ideas for new projects emerge, they often must compete with other equally compelling needs. In the end, the support of top administrators can mean the difference between sustained successes and failed efforts.

Many campuses whose faculty members have international experience and foreign language competency have never made an effort to utilize this hidden resource

CREATE AN INTERNATIONAL ETHOS ON CAMPUS

A high value placed on international and interdisciplinary activities on the campus is one factor associated with successful programs. Most of the programs featured in the previous chapter have prominent profiles on their campuses and are seen as leading forces there for sustaining and improving educational quality. Kalamazoo College, the University of South Carolina's business school, and Worcester Polytechnic Institute each has a campus ethos in which the international dimension is one of the defining characteristics. These institutions have been able to sustain their programs over relatively long periods of time, and campus leaders have adopted international education as a central part of the institution's philosophy.

As a number of these programs attest, one means of achieving visibility for new programs and reflecting the value placed on them is the appropriate use of symbolic actions. One observer notes:

> It is important to have symbols of change—publicity, new titles and administrative units, the distribution of public relations material, conferences, etc., to give people the impression that a change is taking place. Too much can be counterproductive because it looks hollow, but you need enough high-profile symbolic actions to give momentum.[2]

ENGAGE FACULTY COLLEAGUES

No program can be successful without strong faculty support. Individual faculty members must be committed to the value of undertaking these types of projects—and they should be rewarded for their participation and contributions. Not all faculty members are prepared to participate, however. Teaching and research that involve international or interdisciplinary elements often are not highly valued. Moreover, many faculty members lack the training and experience necessary to be significant contributors to efforts at internationalizing the curriculum or developing links with institutions and colleagues abroad.

In many of the programs profiled, faculty development efforts were a major reason cited for the success of the program. Many different strategies have been used to encourage the development of faculty capacity on international issues. Ramapo College provided small grants to purchase books and materials and to hire consultants to help faculty members develop courses and prepare themselves to teach or do research. Bentley College, Worcester Polytechnic Institute, and the University of Michigan have developed ways of getting their faculty members abroad and ensured that their experiences would be integrated into teaching and research after they returned home.

Many campuses whose faculty members have international experience and foreign language competency have never made an effort to utilize this hidden resource. Faculty members at such institutions, however, might in some cases be successfully encouraged to work in teams on course development or research. Those who already have international experience and knowledge can help colleagues develop new approaches to teaching and research. One director of a center for research at a major university describes his efforts at involving faculty members in international activity as a "subversive activity"; he looks for subtle and informal ways of providing incentives for more international research and teaching. He has found that, for example, providing funds for the purchase of large international data sets or for travel to international conferences may stimulate faculty members to consider expanding their range of activities to include an international dimension.

FUNDING IS NECESSARY BUT NOT SUFFICIENT

Curricular innovation—especially when it involves significant faculty development, course development, and travel abroad—can be costly. Most of the programs profiled here benefited from some type of grant or external source of support, at least in the early stages of development. Penn's Lauder Institute and Kalamazoo College received large financial donations from outside benefactors; others competed successfully for grants and were supported by internal campus budgets.

Funding, however, did not always come the first time a proposal was submitted or a budget proposed. Persistence of effort and learning the grantsmanship process were, by many reports, key ingredients of success. Another factor was readiness and preparation. Faced with grant deadlines, institutions too often throw together a proposal at the last minute—then see them fail to produce results. On the other hand, if time has been invested in preparing a proposal and developing the most compelling language and approach, the institution can be ready, when opportunities to seek funds arise, to adapt and submit a proposal with limited changes.

Incorporation into a school or college budget is
one indicator of institutionalization and the
value attached to the program by the larger
university

It is worth noting that most of the programs analyzed did not depend
exclusively on external support. Adequate resources were provided through
regular institutional budgets, thus increasing the likelihood that the program would continue beyond the time constraints usually imposed by
grants. Incorporation into a school or college budget is one indicator of
institutionalization and the value attached to the program by the larger
university

SELECT AN APPROPRIATE CAMPUS HOME

The way international and interdisciplinary activities are best organized
will depend upon such factors as the size of the institution, the scale of
the project, the disciplines and departments involved, and the existing organizational patterns on the campus. The programs profiled in the previous
chapter, as well as others described in the relevant literature, exhibit a
variety of models. Some of the principal ones include:

International centers: Some campuses centralize many of their international initiatives in a campus-wide international center or institute. World
College at Eastern Michigan University is one example. The college serves
as a resource for faculty and curricular development and administers several international programs. UCLA's International Studies and Overseas Program is a support center for efforts to internationalize the curriculum, as
well as a home to virtually all of the areas studies centers and international research activity on the campus.

Colleges: The creation of a separate college or department with its
own admissions procedures, faculty recruitment, and curriculum is another
strategy; an example is Fifth College at the University of California, San
Diego.

Consortia: In some cases, institutions have joined with others to form
consortia that combine resources in the development of international programs, especially for study abroad and exchange programs. The Great
Lakes Consortium for Study Abroad is one of the most noteworthy examples of this approach.

Curricula: Without creating new administrative structures, some
institutions simply focus on changing curricular requirements and options.
Kalamazoo's expectation that students spend time abroad has a powerful
impact on how the whole college functions. The college adapted its calendar and arranges financing for students to achieve this objective. Worcester Polytechnic Institute also focuses on the curriculum, incorporating an

independent field study experience as a primary component of the engineering program.

Student life programs: Recognizing that extracurricular elements can
have a powerful effect on student learning, some campuses have emphasized student activities and student living arrangements as a means to
achieve some internationalization objectives. Pomona College organizes living and eating facilities to encourage groups of students to speak foreign
languages and interact with foreign students on campus. Ramapo College
adopted a policy of increased recruitment of international students and
minorities as a mechanism for enhancing cross-cultural interaction on
campus.

Research centers and institutes: Another means of bringing together
faculty members and students from different disciplines and departments is
organizing curricula and research activities that focus on regions or cultures. Defining a research agenda or undergraduate minor focusing on East
Asia, for example, creates the potential for bringing together groups of students and faculty members from a wide range of disciplines. Area studies
centers and regional research institutes at many research universities typify
this approach, and they frequently make effective use of a strategy of joint
faculty appointments.

THREE CHARACTERISTICS
OF THE MOST SUCCESSFUL PROGRAMS

We conclude with three brief observations about those programs and institutions that seem the *most* successful even among the group profiled here
as vehicles for international education. First, wherever their "home," these
programs tend to have been institutionalized. Many are central to their
campus—its curriculum, its mission, its ethos. They do not depend upon
one person or source of funds and their continuance is widely assumed and
supported.

Secondly, these programs are often multi-dimensional and, in a variety of respects, well integrated. They offer different levels of exposure to
international and global issues—from simple awareness to advanced scholarship—and interdisciplinary collaboration is fundamental to programs and
activities. Multiple projects and activities are parallel yet interlinked, reinforcing each other as the larger institutional emphasis on internationalization.

Thirdly, these programs often have a depth and intensity sufficient to provide substantial numbers of students and faculty with international competence—the ability to function in other cultures. This has been achieved, in part, through a strategy of supporting very well-developed programs in carefully selected areas, rather than trying to cover all regions of the world with a wide range of programs. Hard programmatic choices have been made—of regions, languages, and the like—but the necessary financial resources have also been made readily available to ensure that what *is* done is done well.

1. Burton R. Clark, *The Higher Education System: Academic Organization in Cross-National Perspective* (Berkeley: University of California Press, 1983), 69.
2. Joseph A. Alutto, "Case Discussion: A Framework for Introducing International Perspectives in a School of Management," (paper presented at the AACSB New Deans Seminar, January 21–24, 1990, Scottsdale, Arizona), 8.